Aslan's World

Biblical Images and Themes in *The Lion, the Witch and the Wardrobe*

Angus Menuge

CONCORDIA PUBLISHING HOUSE · SAINT LOUIS

Copyright © 2006 Concordia Publishing House
3558 S. Jefferson Ave., St. Louis, MO 63118-3968
1-800-325-3040 • www.cph.org

Written by Angus Menuge

Edited by Robert C. Baker

Peter Hitchens, "This Is the Most Dangerous Author in Britain," *The Mail on Sunday*, 27 (January 2002) p. 63

"God in the Dock" by C.S. Lewis copyright © 1970 C.S. Lewis Pte. Ltd. Extract reprint by permission.

"After Virtue: A Study in Moral Theory," 2nd edition. (University of Notre Dame Press, 1984) p. 216

Unless otherwise indicated, Scripture quotations are from The Holy Bible, English Standard Version®, copyright © 2001 by Crossway Bibles, a publishing ministry of Good News Publishers, Wheaton, Illinois. Used by permission. All rights reserved.

Scripture quotations marked KJV are from the King James or Authorized Version of the Bible.

This publication may be available in braille, in large print, or on cassette tape for the visually impaired. Please allow 8 to 12 weeks for delivery. Write to the Library for the Blind, 7550 Watson Rd., St. Louis, MO 63119-4409; call toll-free 1-888-215-2455; or visit the Web site: www.blindmission.org.

Manufactured in the United States of America

1 2 3 4 5 6 7 8 9 10   15 14 13 12 11 10 09 08 07 06

Contents

Foreward

    C. S. Lewis said that he wrote *The Lion, the Witch, and the Wardrobe* to help people realize just how wonderful the truths of Scripture—which we are sometimes so familiar with that we take them for granted—really are. So it is appropriate that the book and now the movie send us back to the Bible. Angus Menuge is a Lewis scholar and a fine Biblical thinker in his own right, and he makes a superb guide through both Narnia and the Word of God.

—Gene Edward Veith,
author of *The Soul of The Lion, the Witch and the Wardrobe*

Introduction

Since its first publication in 1950, C. S. Lewis's *The Lion, the Witch and the Wardrobe* has delighted both children and adults with its magical world of talking beasts, mythical creatures, high adventure, and a clear demarcation between Good and Evil. Together with memories from his own childhood, classical mythology, fairy tales from his native British Isles, and clear Christian concepts, Lewis weaves into a beautiful tapestry the colorful and lively world of Narnia—and worlds beyond.

The Lion, the Witch and the Wardrobe was the first volume published in what would later become the seven-book series called The Chronicles of Narnia. Although *The Magician's Nephew* is the earliest in Narnian chronology—detailing Aslan's creation of Narnia—and is now sold as the first volume, for many Lewis scholars and fans *The Lion, the Witch and the Wardrobe* is the key to interpreting the remaining books in the series.

In this Bible study, respected author and professor Angus Menuge draws out and highlights for us the biblical allusions found in *The Lion, the Witch and the Wardrobe*. He does so in such a way that it not only engages Bible study participants, but also leads us deeper into the Scriptures. There we hear not the voice of the great lion Aslan in the world of Narnia, but rather his counterpart in our own. It was He who said,

> Thus it is written, that the Christ should suffer and on the third day rise from the dead, and that repentance and forgiveness of sins should be proclaimed in His name to all nations, beginning from Jerusalem. (Luke 24:46–47)

—The Editor

The Man behind the Books

While many people know that C. S. Lewis wrote the seven children's stories in The Chronicles of Narnia series, few may realize that the stories have a strong Christian element. C. S. Lewis also wrote works of Christian apologetics (works defending and explaining Christianity), such as *Mere Christianity, Miracles*, and *The Problem of Pain*, so it is natural to assume that Lewis wrote children's stories to inculcate Christian doctrine as well.

On the basis of this assumption, some people have a hostile reaction to Lewis's work. Atheists like Philip Pullman confess that they "hate the Narnia books . . . with deep and bitter passion" (quoted in Peter Hitchens, "This Is the Most Dangerous Author in Britain," *The Mail on Sunday*, 27 [January 2002]: p. 63). For Pullman, Lewis is dangerous and even evil because he aims to brainwash unbelievers by imposing Christian ideas on them. Some Christians also think that the Chronicles are too preachy. However, it is important to remember that people cannot simply be told to have faith, since faith is a matter of the heart. The heart trusts in Christ only by the power of the Holy Spirit, who works through the Word of God, not "cleverly devised myths" (2 Peter 1:16) devised by people.

1. Are there legitimate concerns here? Do you think that these assumptions about Lewis's intentions in writing the Chronicles are correct?

At the other extreme, some Christians are so enthusiastic about C. S. Lewis that they seem ready to make him a plaster saint. Some treat his words as if they were an addition to the inspired, inerrant Word of God. Yet Lewis never claimed to be more than an educated layman in the Church of England.

2. Read 1 Corinthians 1:12–17. Why do you think some people revere Lewis so highly? Are there any problems with this attitude?

A Reluctant Convert

Those who think that C. S. Lewis is preachy or condescending toward unbelievers should read his autobiography, *Surprised by Joy*. Although Lewis was raised in a Christian household near Belfast, as a teenager, a number of unfortunate events led him to fall away from the faith. The young Lewis had already suffered the loss of his mother to cancer when he was only nine years old. Then came a succession of English boarding schools, all of which Lewis despised (he compared the first to Belsen, a Nazi concentration camp). At one of these schools, Cherbourg, the matron introduced Lewis to a vague spirituality without a personal God, a moral law, or any real expectations. Lewis, whose childhood understanding of Christianity had been legalistic rather than Gospel-centered, was actually relieved to abandon his faith. Soon he rejected even spirituality in favor of the scientific materialism that was currently in vogue, remaining a proud atheist well into his twenties.

Lewis therefore knew what it was like to be an atheist from the inside. While the natural person is always an enemy of God, Lewis was particularly opposed to the idea of divine direction because, above all else, he disliked being interfered with. Lewis's desire for privacy and autonomy made him fear God as the ultimate interferer, someone who would claim every thought and every moment of our time as His own. Lewis perceived that the Christian is not the owner, occupier, and pilot of his or her soul, but only a steward, entrusted with gifts for service to neighbor and God's glory.

3. In what ways could Lewis's time as an atheist have helped him when he later became a Christian apologist?

Although the Hound of Heaven eventually drew Lewis back to Christ, the process leading to his conversion was a slow one. From an atheist materialist (like Philip Pullman), Lewis became an idealist, believing that some impersonal spiritual principle was needed to justify the ideals of truth, goodness, and beauty that his classical education led him to accept. Then he was shocked by a powerful conviction of sin and found himself praying. He realized that he had violated the will of a personal Lawgiver and that one can pray only to a person, not to an abstraction. Lewis thus became a theist, describing himself as the most reluctant convert in all England. After a motorcycle ride to Whipsnade Zoo, Lewis discovered he was a Christian. From that time on, Lewis devoted his energies to articulating and defending the Christian faith in language that the ordinary layperson could understand. Despite Lewis's brilliance in his academic specialty (medieval and renaissance literature) many of his colleagues resented his popular Christian books—both for their Christianity and their popularity! Lewis continued undeterred.

4. Why do you think Lewis was so determined to communicate Christian ideas to modern people? Do you think it is appropriate for gifted laymen, such as C. S. Lewis or Gene Edward Veith, to bring theology to the masses, or should all theology be handled by specialists?

Lewis never claimed a gift for preaching the Gospel, a call he left to the clergy. But he did discover a gift for Christian apologetics. Lewis found he could prepare people for the Gospel by using apologetics to break down their defenses. His first works of apologetics (such as *The Problem of Pain* and the radio broadcasts that became *Mere Christianity*) showed that standard objections to Christianity do not hold up.

5. Read 1 Peter 3:15 and 2 Corinthians 10:5. What do these passages tell us about the proper role of apologetics? Do you think apologetics is neglected today?

Baptizing the Imagination

Despite his formal apologetics, Lewis came to believe that argument is not always effective. If people really do not want to accept a conclusion, they can reject a premise or debate the meaning of words. They may see an argument as a threat, an attempt to tell them what they should believe. Good stories, by contrast, are more indirect. A good story is *not* preachy. It does not exhort us to believe a statement; it shows the statement's truth by creating a plausible concrete illustration. Then we can see the truth for ourselves.

Of course, we often think of imagination as a realm of make-believe. How could thinking about things that are not really so ("cleverly devised myths" [2 Peter 1:16]) lead us to truth? To be sure, Lewis agreed that some fantasies, such as the school-hero stories popular in his day, deceived people by making them think they could achieve athletic prowess beyond their ability. But the problem with these stories is not that they are fantasy but that they can easily be mistaken for reality. Better stories are about quite different worlds with alien creatures or talking animals, which everyone knows are not real. When humans visit these worlds, their adventures provide an opportunity to show universal truths of the human condition. Lewis's point was that *supposing* there were a world like Narnia, a fallen world of talking beasts, how would Christian truths manifest themselves there? Lewis aimed to awaken readers to the reality of an objective moral law, to show them their sin and their need for a savior.

6. Read Romans 2:14–15 and 1:18, 28–32. Why are Christians confident everyone knows the moral law? Why do some people act as if they do not?

For Lewis, the proper role of imagination is not to wallow in the self-deception of daydreams. Rather, it is to awaken us from the secularizing enchantment of "ordinary life," which can make us doubt whether life has any overarching meaning. In a good story, our minds are focused on concrete instances of universal principles. Lewis's model here is the parables Christ Himself told. When an expert in the law asks Jesus, "Who is my neighbor?" Jesus does not reply with a doctrine of systematic theology. He tells the parable of the Good Samaritan. The expert, and the reader of the parable, no doubt identifies with the priest and Levite who walk by on the other side and is confronted with his own lack of compassion. He is then drawn to the higher example of the Good Samaritan. Perhaps, if his insight rises above moralism, he perceives that his sin makes him just as helpless and unable to save himself as the robbery victim and that Christ Himself is the true Good Samaritan.

7. Why do you think Jesus told so many parables? Why are they so powerful?

Lewis used stories to awaken secular minds to the reality of higher things (the transcendent). He wanted readers to see not only the moral law, but also the possibility of the incarnation, that a loving God could step into His creation to show Himself and to redeem His people from their sin. Lewis did not want to show people their sin only to abandon them to despair. In Aslan, he provides an image of their Savior, Christ. Aslan is a picture of what God might be like incarnate in Narnia.

8. Have you read any stories where the marvelous and the transcendent became more believable? Do they also show our need for a Savior?

Past Watchful Dragons

Stories address the resistance of the heart to direct instruction. To simply tell someone that they have sinned and need forgiveness can provoke all sorts of excuses, evasions, and rationalizations. Our "watchful dragons" quickly spot and attack any threat to the self-righteous portrait we like to paint of ourselves. We are all very good at seeing the specks in other people's eyes while ignoring the logs in our own. Stories can take advantage of this human weakness by showing the sin first in the third person. Then, through the power of reader identification, it can draw us to see the resemblance to ourselves.

9. Read 2 Samuel 12:1–7. What do we learn about the power of story from Nathan? What do you think would have happened if Nathan had rebuked David directly?

Stories are more than information. They are infectious and can change what we value and how we see our vocation. Certainly, stories provide concrete illustrations of virtue and vice, of those who operate faithfully within their vocation and those who usurp the vocation of others. But more than that, they actually form our moral imagination and affect our hearts. In *The Abolition of Man*, Lewis warned of men without chests—people who lack concern for causes and callings higher than their own self-interest. The Chronicles are designed to develop the chest. Stories have this power to change us because we understand ourselves through story. We all have a personal narrative, and this narrative is permeable: it can be changed through outside stories becoming part of our story. The effective parable is not just another story we know about someone else, it helps to define who we are and what we value.

One philosopher who understands this is Alasdair Macintyre, who wrote,

> "Man is in his actions and practice, as well as in his fictions, essentially a story-telling animal. . . . It is through hearing stories about wicked stepmothers, lost children, good but misguided kings, wolves that suckle twin boys, youngest sons who receive no inheritance but must make their own way in the world . . . that children learn . . . both what a child and what a parent is, what the cast of characters may be in the drama into which they have been born. . . . Deprive children of stories and you leave them unscripted, anxious stutterers in their actions as in their words." (*After Virtue: A Study in Moral Theory*, 2nd ed. [University of Notre Dame Press, 1984], p. 216)

10. What do Macintyre's observations tell us about the connection between stories and vocation?

11. Read Luke 15:11–32. How does this illustrate Macintyre's claims? What can we learn about ourselves from both the prodigal son and the elder brother?

The best stories have a universal appeal. Even if they are written at a different time and in a different culture, there is something in the story that transcends those limitations and resonates with the universal human condition. Lewis saw the key to the power of story in its mythic quality, the myth being a point of contact between abstract and concrete. In reading a myth, "you were not knowing, but tasting; but what you were tasting turns out to be a universal principle" ("Myth Became Fact," in *God in the Dock* [Eerdmans, 1970], p. 66).

12. What are some of the universal lessons we can learn from the parable of the prodigal son? How does the parable apply to C. S. Lewis?

Optional DVD Viewing

If there is time, you may now want to show the opening portion of *The Lion, the Witch and the Wardrobe* DVD (scenes 1–4). Otherwise, this can be shown at the beginning of the next class.

Words to Remember

It was fitting to celebrate and be glad, for this your brother was dead, and is alive; he was lost, and is found. Luke 15:32

For Next Time

To prepare for next week's class, all participants should read *The Lion, the Witch and the Wardrobe*, chapters 1–3. Some important questions to think about are these:

1. What does the idea of going through the wardrobe remind us of in the Bible, the Church, or the life of faith?
2. What do we learn about faith and goodness from Lucy's example?
3. What do we learn about the cost of being a witness in an unbelieving world?

Through the Wardrobe

The story focuses on the four Pevensie children, Peter, Susan, Edmund, and Lucy, and takes place during the Second World War. Although the Pevensie children are evacuated from London to the country, they do not find peace. They discover another world, Narnia, through a magic wardrobe, but they do not escape conflict. Indeed, Narnia has a way of clarifying and magnifying moral and spiritual realities. The children are forced to mature very rapidly into warriors, engaging in an epic combat between good and evil.

Lewis did not believe in fantasy as escapism, but as a mode of revelation. The children discover the spiritual battle that is always going on, even in our world, and even in peacetime. Before the children get to Narnia, the seeds of conflict can already be seen in Edmund's resentment of Susan and Peter, who have to function as surrogate parents. When Susan or Peter makes a request of Edmund, he often snaps back. Edmund is seized by the craving for power and autonomy that will be his downfall in Narnia.

13. Read Ephesians 6:10–13. What does this tell us about the war that Christians always face?

War also uproots and disorients. The children are forced to explore a new environment that is not familiar or obvious. Lewis uses disorientation to prepare the protagonists and the reader, opening our minds to new possibilities. Peter notes that the mysterious Professor's house might be full of surprising things and is so large that it might be full of surprising places as well.

14. Read John 14:1–4. Are there any interesting parallels with Lewis's description of the Professor's house?

The Meaning of the Wardrobe

Forced inside by the rain, the Pevensie children explore the Professor's house, and Lucy discovers a magic wardrobe. Most of the time, the wardrobe has an ordinary wooden back. But sometimes and for some people, it serves as a portal into Narnia. The portal cannot be opened by human choice. If it opens, it is because Aslan is calling people out of our world and into a new role in Narnia. The call is not to a vacation, a place to rest from everyday responsibilities. On the contrary, the tasks become harder and the burdens become heavier.

15. Read 1 Thessalonians 4:11–12 and 2 Thessalonians 3:6–13. What do they say to the person who sees a life of faith only as a refuge from the world's struggles?

16. Read 1 Corinthians 7:20. Are our callings a matter of preference and choice? Do we control them?

When Lucy goes through the wardrobe, she discovers a whole new world. As she moves back through it, she recognizes that it must be enormous. Later, when the other children discover Narnia, they realize that it is all right to take the fur coats because they would not be leaving the wardrobe. In a sense, the whole country of Narnia was inside it. This is a paradox, because Narnia is much bigger than the wardrobe. Lewis thereby suggests some important Christian truths. In a stable in Bethlehem, an infinite and holy God took on flesh and dwelt among us. When we receive Holy Communion, in, with, and under the bread and wine, that same God is present in His body and blood. When we open a Bible, a medium-size book that weighs a few pounds provides access to a transcendent realm; it is the very Word of God. Even if we worship in a modern church that looks rather like a dentist's office, we join with all the company of heaven. With God, the inside is often bigger than the outside.

17. Read Colossians 1:15–20 and John 1:3, 14. What is remarkable about the fact that all of these verses refer to Christ? What kind of Creator do we have?

There are many other meanings suggested by going through the wardrobe. It reminds us that even ordinary books, books that have not been divinely inspired, cause us to forget ourselves and open us to a whole new world of meaning. Every time we become more enthralled with the world of the book than our ongoing concerns, the wardrobe is open. The imagination is shown to be more than a vehicle for idle daydreams. It is a way of accessing truth that transcends our immediate experience. We discover times, places, and people we have never met. We may also discover the marvelous accounts of miracles—signs and wonders—that we have not personally witnessed. Our mind is thereby opened to the possibility of the transcendent, to higher things that not only lie behind, but also interpenetrate what we call real life. Lewis himself said that a book by the Scottish poet and theologian George MacDonald, *Phantastes*, had baptized his own imagination with the idea of holiness, of the radical otherness and moral perfection of the divine.

18. Read Revelation 1:10–18 and Matthew 28:1–6. How do these verses communicate holiness? Why do we all, as sinners, fear the holy? What comfort does the Gospel provide?

19. Beyond good practical advice, do you see any theological significance in the repeated reminder that it is unsafe to shut the wardrobe door?

17

Trust, Deception, and Goodness

Lucy is amazed by the otherness of Narnia. Although she is somewhat afraid, she has the courage to explore Narnia. From the very beginning, Lucy, the youngest of the Pevensie children, has an openness to higher things. Perhaps she already has faith (we may speculate that she has been baptized, or even that passage through the wardrobe symbolizes Baptism). On the other hand, she recognizes that she can leave Narnia, and the wardrobe, if necessary. This might suggest the natural person's fear of being put to death so that the new person in Christ can appear. Or it might be that though Lucy has a baptismal faith, it has not been nurtured, and she lacks catechetical instruction to know what to hold on to.

20. Read Romans 6:3–4 and Matthew 13:3–9, 18–23. What do these verses tell us about our resistance to faith commitment?

Whatever the state of Lucy's faith, she is truthful, is kind, and implicitly trusts others. When she meets Mr. Tumnus, she shows no signs of suspicion or doubt about his character. In these days of child abduction and unspeakable abuse, it must be emphasized that Lucy's trust of a complete stranger in an alien environment is not a good model for children in our own world. Even in Narnia, Lucy's actions are imprudent. For although he seems welcoming and kind, Mr. Tumnus is in the service of the White Witch, a usurping enchantress, the Satan figure of Narnia. She makes it always winter and never Christmas. Behind the offer of tea and snacks is a kidnapping plot.

21. Read 2 Corinthians 11:13–15. What warning do these verses contain about those in league with Satan? Why are they not always obvious even to Christians?

Any time we realize we are in danger, we tend to react by fight or flight, by resisting or fleeing the threat. Most people who discover they have been kidnapped do not respond like Lucy! But then, most kidnappers are more ruthless and callous than Mr. Tumnus. Although Narnia has been under snow and ice for one hundred years, and Tumnus has known only oppression and fear, Lucy's honest and trusting nature awakens his conscience. When he realizes how low he has sunk, he bursts into tears. His conscience is troubled even further by the portrait of his upright father, whom he knows would not have acted as he. But more than anything, it is Lucy herself who conquers Mr. Tumnus by suggesting she couldn't hand him over to the Witch. Plotting evil in the abstract is one thing; harming an innocent young girl in the forest proves intolerable.

22. Read Romans 12:17–21. How do these verses apply to Lucy? Why should we repay evil with good? How is this response rooted in God's love for us?

Lucy's goodness and faith in Mr. Tumnus's underlying good character is like a bright mirror in which he sees his sin and realizes how far he has fallen. But Lucy is also gracious, freely and fully forgiving Mr. Tumnus for his wicked designs, and showing concern for his welfare now that he has rejected the White Witch's commands.

23. Read Luke 17:1–4. How seriously does Jesus take sin? How willing should we be to forgive it? Read Proverbs 15:1. What can we learn from the fact that Lucy calls Mr. Tumnus to repentance *without* harsh language?

Edmund and the Wardrobe

When people hear a wonderful message from a reliable source, they find it both hard to believe and hard to disbelieve. It is hard to believe because we are all enchanted by the familiar. Although even the familiar is wonderful if we can see how it reflects God's glory, we tend to become jaded. Familiarity may not always breed contempt, but it often leads to a weary expectation that nothing exciting or new will happen. At the same time, it is troubling if the source of the

19

wonderful message is trustworthy, since that creates a presumption of truth. No matter how bored we may be at times, we still find ourselves hoping for something more. So we are reluctant to close the door forever on the marvelous.

This is why, when Lucy returns, her claim to have discovered another world through the wardrobe is greeted with a complex reaction. Edmund, who likes to pretend he is an adult, and who longs to usurp Peter and Susan's authority, dismisses Lucy as crazy. Susan and Peter, who are kinder, also find it hard to believe Lucy because she claims to have been in Narnia for hours, yet only moments have elapsed in our world. But Lucy sticks to her story, and her excitement is infectious. Honesty, consistency, and enthusiasm evidently count for something. So despite their doubts, the other children do consent to check the wardrobe out. This time it is closed; they can see the back of it, and to be certain, Peter knocked on it with his knuckles, as if the children almost believed Lucy's story.

24. Read Luke 24:13–27. Are there any interesting parallels between Lucy and the women of verses 22–23, and between the other children and the two men on the road to Emmaus?

Now Lucy must learn the hard lesson Christians face: of sticking to a story one believes in the face of incredulity and ridicule. The other children think Lucy is either lying or going mad, and Edmund mocks her mercilessly. This takes its toll, because Lucy does not yet have that great benefit of the Church, a community of fellow believers to support her. This causes her to doubt whether she had seen the faun in Narnia, supposing that it might have been a dream.

25. Read Acts 26:13–29. How are Lucy's trials similar to Paul's experience before Agrippa?

Lucy has no power of her own to call Edmund into Narnia or to make him believe in Narnia. But Aslan is still calling Lucy, and even though she did not intend to enter it, she is drawn inside again, and this leads Edmund to follow, intent on harassing her about Narnia.

20

Thus Edmund discovers Narnia. Edmund's pride prevents him from full repentance: he says he is sorry only because he does not like being alone in a strange new world.

Narnia has a way of intensifying the spiritual condition of those who enter it. Lucy's innocence and trust conquers Mr. Tumnus's deception, but Edmund's pride and desire to usurp legitimate power make him prey *to* the deception of the White Witch. Unable to accept the truth about his vocation as a younger, dependent brother, he is vulnerable to the Witch's manipulative lies.

26. Review 2 Corinthians 11:14, and consider the description of the White Witch. How is it suggestive of Satan? What is ironic about her use of a sleigh?

Optional DVD Viewing

You may now want to continue with *The Lion, the Witch and the Wardrobe* DVD (scenes 5–8). Otherwise, this can be shown at the beginning of the next class.

Words to Remember

But even if you should suffer for righteousness' sake, you will be blessed. Have no fear of them, nor be troubled, but in your hearts regard Christ the Lord as holy, always being prepared to make a defense to anyone who asks you for a reason for the hope that is in you; yet do it with gentleness and respect, having a good conscience, so that, when you are slandered, those who revile your good behavior in Christ may be put to shame. 1 Peter 3:14–16.

For Next Time

To prepare for next week's class, all participants should read *The Lion, the Witch and the Wardrobe*, chapters 4–6. Some important questions to think about are these:

1. What do we learn about temptation and Satan's deceptions from Turkish delight?

2. How does the Professor show that it is not logic, but a secular worldview that blinds people to the transcendent?
3. Beyond the fact that it is cold in Narnia, what do you think is significant about the fact that the children put on the fur coats they find in the wardrobe?

Faith, Doubt, and Logic

Edmund is quite defenseless before the White Witch. It is evident that his education has been secular (he has no idea what the Witch means by the phrase "son of Adam"), and so he has no tools to help him identify and reject satanic evil. Edmund is naturally afraid of the Witch's imposing, imperious character, but he has no weapons to defend himself with. The Witch realizes, but Edmund does not, that he and his siblings are connected to a prophecy concerning the end of the Witch's reign and the restoration of Narnia. The Witch aims to thwart the prophecy and rises to destroy Edmund, but then appears to relent.

A first-time reader of the book might initially believe that the Witch has had a change of heart, that she is sorry for Edmund. Indeed, she projects a persona of warmth and kindness by appearing sympathetic to Edmund and offering to share her warm mantle with him. Then the Witch provides a hot drink, made by magic, and asks Edmund to name his favorite food. As Edmund becomes more and more comfortable and his senses are gratified, he starts to suspend any critical thinking about what the Witch is up to. He ought to be concerned about why the same person who looked as if she meant to kill him is now being so nice. He should be considering whether she has an ulterior motive, and he should be cautious about giving out information to a stranger. But he forgets all of this as her enchantment grows stronger.

27. Read 1 Peter 5:8–9. What advice does Peter give that would help Christians avoid Edmund's predicament?

Turkish Delight

Edmund's favorite food is Turkish delight, a gelatinous confectionary made with starch and sugar and usually flavored with rosewater— making it pink—cut into cubes, and dusted with sugar. The author of this Bible study used to receive a round sandalwood box of Turkish delight for Christmas. It is a delicacy for those with a sweet tooth, and most children find it difficult to have just one piece, even though too much of it can obviously ruin one's appetite for wholesome food.

These characteristics make Turkish delight an apt, if a little obscure, metaphor for the allure and addiction of sin. Edmund is so consumed by the desire for it that he forgets about normal prudence and happily tells the Witch about his siblings. Without realizing what he is doing, Edmund is already beginning to betray his brother and sisters. In the process, he is falling under the control of the Turkish delight. We learn with a shock that this Turkish delight is bewitched and that, if they were not stopped from eating it, those tasting this magical treat would continue eating it until it killed them.

28. Read Genesis 3:1–19. How is the fruit described (v. 6)? How does Satan deceive Eve? Are there any important similarities with the account of Edmund and the Turkish delight?

29. Read 1 John 2:15–17 and Romans 6:20–23. How do these passages comment on Edmund's sin and its inevitable consequences, absent a savior?

The uncomfortable truth is that all of us, even Christians, are surrounded and tempted by "Turkish delight." It may be that a liking for fine food and wine tempts us to gluttony or that a craving for intimacy and romance tempts us to promiscuity. But even if we can resist these urges, there is the desire for status and power. We are always seeking praises among other people, and would like a more exalted position at the table so that we can lord it over others. We tell ourselves this is the recognition we deserve and do not see how full of pride we are becoming.

30. Read James 3:13–18. What does the difference between worldly and heavenly wisdom tell us about our "Turkish delight"?

Like a drug addict, Edmund is now hooked on Turkish delight and ready to do anything to get more of it. He is pulled away from his true vocation as younger brother, and he starts to become selfish and proud, just like the White Witch. Wanting Edmund to bring his siblings to Narnia, she promises whole rooms of Turkish delight and that he will be prince and later king of Narnia. Edmund does not realize that the Witch is lying and starts to live in a fabricated dreamland. Just as the Witch is not really the legitimate queen of Narnia, but a usurping tyrant, Edmund's desire for independence from his siblings is magnified into a lust for power over a whole world. When the Witch offers titles to his siblings, Edmund's swelling pride makes him say, in effect, that they are unimportant. All the while, the Witch is manipulating Edmund's desires so that she can get what she wants. When Edmund meets Lucy and finds out how others view the Witch, he is shocked, but unable to conquer his sinful desires, he starts to tell himself and others convenient lies. In fact, his sin is making him sick to his stomach.

31. Read John 8:42–47. Why does the devil want to make people liars?

Logic!

Back on this side of the wardrobe, Edmund is a much worse person than before. In the past, his desire for power over others had appeared in the form of bullying smaller children. But now Edmund, who is siding more and more with the Witch, becomes a traitor to his own family. It starts in a small way, with his betrayal of Lucy. Lucy is delighted that Edmund will be able to confirm her Narnia story but becomes utterly distraught when he lets her down. Edmund lies, saying that Lucy and he were only playing a game, and then treats her with condescension. Edmund's worsening nastiness is not lost on Peter, but he feels compelled to conclude that Lucy is either going mad or becoming a terrible liar.

Susan and Peter think these are the only logical explanations and bring them to the Professor. He surprises them by pointing out that their conclusions rest on a truncated logic, one that fails to consider all of the relevant possibilities. He calls attention to what logicians call the fallacy of false alternatives: the argument that "Jack is not a Democrat; therefore, he is a Republican" is a bad one because it falsely assumes that there are only two political parties to choose from. The conclusion that Lucy is either lying or mad rests on the assumption that she cannot be telling the truth, which is never considered. Peter and Susan only consider normal solutions, excluding the transcendent from the outset in much the same way that many will exclude the possibility of miracles or even intelligent design *before* examining the evidence. When they do consider the possibility that Lucy is telling the truth, it turns out that the two rival explanations are not well supported by evidence. Lucy is known to be very honest, much more so than Edmund, and her demeanor and cogent speech show she is not mad. The problem is not logic but a secular worldview that is closed to the transcendent.

32. Read 1 Corinthians 2:14. Why is a secular worldview closed to higher things?

The Professor's argument is a beautiful preparation for Lewis's later argument in *Mere Christianity* about the person of Christ. Once someone has accepted the reliability of the New Testament as history (Jesus is not a legend but a historical figure of flesh and blood), he or she must confront Jesus' claims to be God (forgiving sins in general, having authority over the Law, working miracles, and praying to God the Father as His personal Father). When a human being claims to be God, the only possibilities are that he is lying, deranged, or telling the truth. But even unbelievers like Bertrand Russell and Gandhi conceded the wisdom of Jesus' moral teaching, and Jesus' miracles evidence more than a normal man. When we actually consider the possibility that Jesus is God, we see it is the one best supported by the evidence. Faith is, of course, God-given trust of the heart and not merely intellectual assent. But arguments are important to show that what we believe in faith is objectively true, for it is the object of faith that saves.

33. Read John 20:24–28. What does Thomas conclude from a fair examination of the evidence?

34. Read 1 Corinthians 15:1–20. How does Paul emphasize that the Christian faith is founded on objective, historical fact that can be checked out? Why is this important in showing that Christianity is not, like many other religions, an unverifiable myth?

A Royal Calling

Although the children may remain skeptical and do not choose to examine the wardrobe again, they are drawn in all the same, against their will, because of a party of sightseers. Viewed as a metaphor for coming to faith, Lewis makes it clear that God is the one who calls and that our wills are powerless to choose Him.

35. Reread Luke 14:16–24. If the banquet is the kingdom of heaven, what is astonishing about verses 21 and 23? Why do you think Lewis said of his own conversion that, paradoxically, divine compulsion was liberation?

But God does not call people to faith merely to comfort them. He calls people into service. Yet though God wants our work, since it is through our vocations that we serve others, he elevates all work by promoting believers into adopted members of His royal family. Lewis suggests this idea in a beautifully understated way. The children take the coats in the wardrobe, ostensibly just to protect themselves from the cold.

But of course it is cold because Narnia is in the grip of the Witch. The winter is symbolic of her reign: the cold is oppressive and forces believers in Aslan underground; the uniform whiteness of the snow evokes the suppression of individuality and life by the Witch's totalitarian demand for conformity to her will. The coats, therefore, suggest protection from the Witch's oppressive power. We also learn that they had the appearance of royal clothing. The fact that the coats offer protection against Satan's power suggests the free gift of Christ's righteousness that Christians receive in Baptism. The fact that the coats are too big captures the idea that God calls us into work beyond our current preferences and capacities. Furthermore, He sends gifts to enable us to complete our tasks. But the mention of royal robes is clearly a reference to the royal priesthood of all those adopted into the family of God.

36. Read Galatians 3:26–27 and 1 Peter 2:9–10. How do these verses give a reading of Lewis's metaphor of the fur coats?

Gifts can be used well or badly. Because of his prior commitment to the White Witch, Edmund, like Judas, shows himself to be unworthy of his coat. When Edmund gives away the fact that he had been in Narnia before, and Peter rebukes him harshly, Edmund does not repent but nurses his resentment by plotting revenge. When they discover that Mr. Tumnus has been arrested by the Witch, all the children must consider what to do about it. Edmund, of course, has no interest in helping. Susan points out how dangerous it is and how unprepared they are for an adventure. But when Lucy insists that they must do something to help Mr. Tumnus, Susan and Peter agree. They are already changing, growing up into the vocations Aslan has called them to.

37. Read Ephesians 4:11–16. How do Christians "grow up"?

Part of the children's growth involves no longer leaning on their own understanding (Proverbs 3:5). They start to discern signs of God's calling and to trust that He will provide. When a robin appears and seems to want them to follow, Edmund raises skeptical doubts, but Peter leads by faith in the robin's goodness.

38. Read 2 Corinthians 5:7. If "sight" means the certainty of our natural reason, what is the role of faith in Christian leadership?

Optional DVD Viewing

You may now want to continue with *The Lion, the Witch and the Wardrobe* DVD (scenes 9–11). Otherwise, this can be shown at the beginning of the next class.

Words to Remember

You are no longer strangers and aliens, but you are fellow citizens with the saints and members of the household of God, built on the foundation of the apostles and prophets, Christ Jesus Himself being the cornerstone. Ephesians 2:19–20

For Next Time

To prepare for next week's class, all participants should read *The Lion, the Witch and the Wardrobe*, chapters 7–10. Some important questions to think about are these:

1. Is there a biblical parallel with the loyal and faithful Beavers?
2. How do the children react when they first hear of Aslan? Why are there different reactions?
3. What is significant about Father Christmas's gifts? Do they have a biblical parallel?

Aslan Is on the Move

When the robin flies away and leaves the children, it might seem that their trust was ill-founded. But the robin has faithfully done his work, leading the children to Mr. Beaver. Again, they are uncertain if they can trust him. Edmund is the most skeptical because his perception of goodness has been distorted by his allegiance to the White Witch. The others are unsure but have a clearer perception of the goodness of Mr. Beaver. Their spiritual eyes are starting to discern the difference between good and evil more clearly.

Reassured that Mr. Beaver was sent by Mr. Tumnus, they follow him into the shade, and he confides that Aslan is on the move. The deep emotional reaction of the children shows us that *Aslan* is a powerful name that elicits the responses we reserve for the divine. Although the children have not yet seen Aslan with their own eyes, Mr. Beaver's statement starts to change them.

39. Read Hebrews 4:12–13. How do these verses suggest an interpretation of the children's reaction?

The children do not all react to Mr. Beaver's words in the same way. Each child senses something deep within them, but while Peter, Susan, and Lucy have a variety of uplifting experiences, Edmund is horrified. It is in just this way that Christ appears as beautiful Savior to those who fall on His mercy, but as a terrifying judge to those who have rejected Him in order to assert their own willful independence. The tragedy is that freedom from Christ is not freedom at all, but slavery to Satan.

40. Read John 3:16–21 and John 8:34–36. How do these verses explain the different reactions the children have to Aslan's name and that people have to Christ and the true meaning of freedom?

The Last Prophets and the Lion of Judah

After hearing about Aslan, the perception of the children is altered. The word of hope opens the hearts of everyone except Edmund so they were enabled to trust Mr. Beaver. As the Word of God is a means of grace, the Holy Spirit works through those means and creates trust in the heart. Peter, Susan, and Lucy are happy to accept Mr. Beaver as an ambassador of Aslan and congratulate him on his dam. But Edmund's perception is drawn elsewhere by his allegiance to the Witch, so that he alone notices the two small hills around her palace. Out of fear of Aslan, Edmund is drawn closer to the White Witch and is consumed by deceitful thoughts about Turkish delight and ruling his own siblings as subjects.

41. Read Romans 8:5. How does it serve to explain the difference between Edmund's mindset and that of his siblings?

The children do not yet understand that Aslan has called them into Narnia to fulfill his providential plan to restore Narnia. But the Beavers know. Mrs. Beaver is amazed to see the children and is grateful to participate in the unfolding of these events. Like the last prophets who overlap the Old and New Testaments, the Beavers have kept the faith that Aslan would save Narnia from the Witch, and now they are seeing the fulfillment of prophecy unfold before their eyes.

42. Read Luke 1:67–80 and 2:25–32. How are the Beavers like Zechariah and Simeon?

The Beavers' house is the first place the children have experienced in Narnia that evokes a Christian household—warm, comfortable, peaceful, and well-ordered. After dinner, the Beavers tell the children more about the White Witch and Aslan. We learn that the White Witch turns people into stone, suggesting that she takes away the freedom and life of faith by producing apostate hearts hardened in rejection of God.

43. Read Hebrews 3:12–15 and Ezekiel 11:19. What do these verses tell us about the hearts of believers and unbelievers?

Of course Edmund wants to know if the Witch can turn Aslan to stone. Afraid of Aslan's judgment, he deceives himself with the fantasy that Aslan can be destroyed. But Aslan is no ordinary lion. His father is the Emperor-beyond-the-Sea. If the Emperor is like God the Father, Aslan is like the Son of God. In a world of talking beasts, it makes sense that the God figure is the king of beasts. Aslan reminds us that one of Jesus' titles is *Lion of Judah*.

44. Read Genesis 49:9–10; Hosea 5:14–6:2; and Revelation 5:1–10. How is the image of God as a lion both terrifying and comforting? How can God have both of these dimensions?

Above all we learn that Aslan is not "safe"; although, he is good and he is the sovereign. We learn that Aslan, like God, cannot be domesticated. God is not a projection of human desires, a puppet or a pet to console us on our own sinful terms. He is not our creature; rather, we are His creatures and should therefore live in complete dependence on His mercy. Lewis communicates the important and countercultural idea that God is a holy being whose ways are above our own and to whom we must learn to submit our will, obeying Him out of gratitude for His many undeserved blessings.

45. Read Isaiah 40:13–31. How do these verses destroy human arrogance and restore humility before God?

Self-Deception and Betrayal

Edmund's hankering for forbidden fruits makes him no longer able to appreciate the daily bread that God provides. That is why while the other children enjoy the wholesome food at the Beavers' house, Edmund's mind is fixated on Turkish delight. The more Edmund learns of Aslan, the more he is afraid. While Mr. Beaver explains the prophecy about two kings and two queens at Cair Paravel, Edmund slips away and heads for the White Witch's palace. Because of his complicity with the White Witch, he starts to construct a fictional world based on his desires in order to console himself. Although he resents his siblings, he does not really want to turn them to stone and begins to convince himself that she will not truly harm them. Yet he remains in conflict with even this false hope because he deeply senses her evil nature.

47. Read 1 John 2:9–11. What is the connection between Edmund's rejecting his siblings and rejecting God? What remedy is provided by the well-known verses in 1 John 1:8–9?

It is significant that Edmund leaves his coat behind at the Beavers' house. This symbolizes his rejection of grace, his preference for his own will over the righteousness of Christ. He discovers that no road lay before him because he has rejected the one who is "the way, and the truth, and the life" (John 14:6). Edmund becomes cold, miserable, and lonely now that he has also rejected the fellowship of the Beavers and even his own flesh and blood. He can console himself only with fantasies about being king, while absurdly blaming Peter for his discomfort. The palace, when he reaches it, is frightening, not comforting. Deep down, Edmund is so afraid of Aslan and so troubled in his conscience, that even a stone lion paralyzes him. When he finally realizes it is only a statue, Edmund tries to convince himself that the Witch turned Aslan to stone, and to comfort himself with sacrilegious doodling on the lion's face. But the tactic does not work: a face like Aslan's (it is, of course, a different lion) proves too noble to be fun to mess with.

47. Read Galatians 6:7–8. How do these verses comment on the futility of Edmund's actions?

48. Read Matthew 13:11–15. How do these verses comment on the difference between Edmund and his siblings?

Indeed, Edmund's perception of reality is thoroughly distorted by his sinful desires. After deceiving himself that Aslan has been turned to stone, he overlooks a wolf who is very much alive. Wolves are, of course, common symbols for the enemies of Christ. But Edmund has blinded himself to the truth. He expects the Witch to be pleased to see him, but she is furious that he has come alone. He is now so concerned about being liked by the Witch that he betrays the whereabouts of his own siblings. Perhaps even Edmund is shocked by the menace in her voice when the Witch commands the dwarf to make ready her sleigh using the bell-less harness. If she means no harm, as Edmund tried to make himself believe, why is she so concerned that her arrival will be unnoticed?

49. Read Ephesians 4:20–27. What are the connections between deceitfulness and sin, truth and holiness? How is Edmund's self-deception leading him into worsening acts of betrayal?

Equipped to Serve

Meanwhile, the other children help the Beavers get ready for their trek to the Stone Table, where they hope to see Aslan. They are aware that the White Witch will try to stop them, and there is a humorous dialogue between the majority, who think they must leave immediately, and Mrs. Beaver, who wants to make sure they have adequate provisions. Lewis subtly suggests that a life of faith does not mean the rejection of common prudence. This theme is reinforced by Mr. Beaver leading them to a hiding place, reminiscent of the catacombs in which the Early Church met to avoid persecution. Christians may be martyred for faithful proclamation of the Gospel truth, but they are not called to throw away their lives. The crosses that God sends us must be endured and embraced, but we are not asked to seek additional crosses of our own choice. Since Aslan himself has called them to the Stone Table, faithfully following their vocation requires using all of their wits to stay alive. Natural gifts—the mind and body and what nourishes them—are not to be despised, and they are glad later to have the bread knife!

50. Read Proverbs 8:1–21; Matthew 10:16; Romans 12:2; and 1 Corinthians 14:20. What do these verses tell us about the importance of wisdom and prudence in the life of Christians?

It soon seems as if their provisions were in vain. They hear jingling bells, which the Witch usually uses on her sleigh. However, it is not the Witch but the one she has impersonated, Father Christmas. This is very significant, because, for one hundred years, it has been always winter and never Christmas. Christmas signifies the beginning of the incarnation of the Son of God. In Narnia, it means that the Son of the Emperor-beyond-the-Sea is coming to Narnia and that all of the old prophecies will be fulfilled.

Interestingly, Father Christmas's reindeer are brown, not white, and he is wearing a colorful red robe. Here and elsewhere, Lewis characterizes those of the household of faith as brightly colored, emphasizing their individuality and fullness of life, in contrast to the whiteness of the Witch and her realm in which death and anonymous slavery reign. Colors are also suggestive of the richness of the gifts Christ bestows. For in addition to natural gifts, there are also spiritual gifts. God always equips those He calls. Father Christmas gives each of the three children special gifts to aid in their assigned vocation. Since these gifts grant protection against the White Witch, the Satan of Narnia, it is clear the gifts are not merely physical. Peter receives a shield and a sword, Susan a bow and arrows and a horn to call for help, and Lucy a vial of healing elixir and a dagger.

51. Read Ephesians 6:10–18. What specific spiritual armor does God provide? What interpretation is there for Peter's shield and sword? What interpretations could we suggest for Susan's and Lucy's gifts?

The girls are told that they are not to fight in the battle. Lucy protests her bravery. But courage is a natural virtue, and the issue is whether God chooses to bestow the same spiritual gifts on men and women. Perhaps Lewis's real point is that men and women have different vocations in the Church. His main point is surely not that women should not serve in the military.

52. Read Romans 12:3–8. What do we learn about God's distribution of gifts?

Optional DVD Viewing

You may want to continue with *The Lion, the Witch and the Wardrobe* DVD (scenes 12–17). Otherwise, this can be shown at the beginning of the next class.

Words to Remember

There are varieties of gifts, but the same Spirit; and there are varieties of service, but the same Lord. 1 Corinthians 12:4–5.

For Next Time

To prepare for next week's class, all participants should read *The Lion, the Witch and the Wardrobe*, chapters 11–14. Some important questions to think about are these:

1. What do we learn about the difference between God and Satan from the contrasts between the characters of the White Witch and Aslan?
2. Why does Peter have to win his spurs?
3. What is the significance of the Deep Magic?
4. What biblical truths are conveyed by the portrayal of the death of Aslan?

Promise Breakers and Promise Keepers

Jesus tells us to judge character by its fruits: "every healthy tree bears good fruit, but the diseased tree bears bad fruit" (Matthew 7:17). The supreme example is the contrast between God and Satan. James says that "Every good gift and every perfect gift is from above, coming down from the father of lights with whom there is not variation or shadows due to change" (James 1:17). God is a promise keeper. When His inspired prophets foretold a coming savior, He made it come to pass, just as He had said. This is why we know our trust in Him is well-founded. We are not clinging to a rope whose other end is loose; we are tethered to Christ, our rock and our Redeemer: "We have this as a sure and steadfast anchor of the soul" (Hebrews 6:19). Satan is not only a liar, but "the father of lies" (John 8:44). He "disguises himself as an angel of light" (2 Corinthians 11:14). He has no real gifts but tempts people to destruction by vain and empty hopes. Satan is the promise breaker *par excellence*, who offers people the world but wants to take their soul.

When Edmund asks for more Turkish delight, he discovers that the White Witch had no intention of keeping her side of the bargain. She had induced a sinful addiction to get Edmund to do her will, but now she no longer needs him. He is horrified to learn that the Witch's plan is to kill his siblings. Satan, too, "was a murderer from the beginning" (John 8:44).

53. Read Matthew 7:24–27 and 16:26. What do these verses tell us about the importance of building our faith on the right foundation?

Repentance

When the White Witch leaves on her sleigh, the journey is awful for Edmund. Partly, this is because he has no coat: he lacks the protection of Christ's righteousness against the Witch's power, symbolized by the driving snow. But Edmund also suffers the misery of disillusionment. He realizes the Witch never intended to make him king. Indeed, every promise she ever made to him now sounded silly. Edmund's eyes have been opened to the horrible truth about the Witch, and as soon as he rejects her, he is able to see the truth about his siblings. For the first time, he would actually rather be with them.

54. Read Matthew 27:1–5. How is Edmund like and unlike Judas?

Edmund is not yet a believer in Aslan, but he is starting to repent of his allegiance to the White Witch. As he does so, he begins to see the truth of the moral law more clearly. When the Witch discovers a party of creatures enjoying a feast laid by Father Christmas, she turns them to stone. No longer under her grip, Edmund experiences sympathy for someone (or some things, in this case) other than himself. The essence of Edmund's sin, like all sin, was his self-love. While consumed with the desire for personal advancement, he had become more and more callous and cruel, just like the Witch. Now that he has rejected her, he starts to see the plight of others more objectively and even finds compassion. But there is something more. As Edmund's heart starts to thaw, so does the Witch's winter. No longer bothering with deception, the Witch continues to treat him as a slave, but Edmund is relieved to see signs of new life.

55. Read Matthew 3:1–12. What is the relationship between repentance and faith? How does John the Baptist "prepare the way"?

But it is not only Edmund who is called to repentance. When his siblings meet Aslan at the Stone Table, Aslan's first question is about missing Edmund. Of course Aslan knows the answer, as God knew the answer when He asked Adam and Eve what they had done (Genesis 3). The purpose of the question is not to elicit information but to call for a confession. Peter is moved by the power of Aslan's word to say that Edmund's betrayal of them was partly his own fault because he had been angry at Edmund.

56. Read Romans 3:10–20. How do these verses show that even those, such as Peter, who are upright by human standards still need a savior?

Confession should be followed by absolution, and readers may be confused that Aslan does not speak words of forgiveness to Peter. However, they can all see by the look in Aslan's eyes that he has granted forgiveness. Aslan's expression shows that, though no sin is excusable, he will not count Peter's sin against him. Aslan's consistently gracious gaze suggests the constancy of God's love toward us, despite our failings. What the children do not yet know is the terrible price God chose to pay to make us right with him. When Lucy asks if anything can be done to save Edmund, she has no idea that Aslan himself must die in his place.

57. Read Romans 3:21–31. How can Aslan treat Peter as righteous even though he is a sinner?

Signs of Change

Repentance is a kind of thawing in the human heart as it turns away from sin. Through the work of the Law, even unbelievers like Edmund can be brought to their senses and see evil for what it is. But this does not by itself create faith. Edmund's heart is prepared for the Gospel, but he does not yet know his savior. On the other hand, there are signs of regeneration everywhere. The snow thaws, representing the waning of the Witch's power. Water begins to run in torrents. Colors return: first green and then blossoms and flowers. There is bird song, and the trees burst forth with life after a century of dormancy.

Even the Witch's dwarf realizes this is more than a thaw: it is spring, a new season, like the inception of a new age or a new kingdom, signifying the end of her reign.

58. Read Romans 8:22–23. How could this passage provide a commentary on the account of the new spring?

59. Read Joel 2:21–22. Although this passage refers to the recovery of the land from the invasion of locusts, how does it tie in with the renewal of creation in general? Why do you think the Old Testament writers used the idea of the renewal of the land as a picture of our salvation?

There is more to new life than the spring. There is also feasting and celebration. Father Christmas begins to bring his gifts, reminding us that we have a gracious God who freely gives us undeserved righteousness. Aslan himself asks for a feast to be prepared. Although the text does not say it in so many words, the feast is obviously in honor of the coming of Aslan, the king of beasts, who will save Narnia from the White Witch. In Aslan's face, there is a sense of celebration and yet also sadness; they should feast now, yet a bitter trial is imminent.

60. Read Mark 2:19–20. What does this text suggest is the reason for a feast? How does it capture both the joy and sadness of the occasion?

At an individual level, we see this new life reflected in the children's growth into their callings. When Susan is chased by a wolf into a tree, Aslan does not allow any of the talking beasts to fight but calls Peter. Before Peter is made king, he must first show himself to be a worthy knight. Since wolves are figures of satanic deception and Peter's sword is a spiritual weapon, a sword of truth, it is Peter's faith that is tested by his first battle. The battle is not so much with the wolf as with himself. Naturally, Peter lacks courage, but he must trust in the one who calls him to do what is right. Peter's wrestling with the wolf is reminiscent of the Christian's wrestling with the old Adam. Despite his weakness, with Aslan's help, Peter conquers his foe and is knighted.

61. Read Romans 7:14–25. What does this text tell us about a Christian's struggle with sin?

We also see how the office changes the officeholder, that God makes those He calls grow up into their vocations. God's assessment of who has the requisite gifts is often quite different from our own. Peter did not think he had it in him, but Aslan knew otherwise.

62. Read 1 Samuel 16:6–7. What does God know about our suitability for a vocation that we do not?

The Deep Magic

Thinking that she can make the prophecy about the four thrones at Cair Paravel fail, the Witch decides to kill Edmund. Of course, this is absurd, because the prophecy is a promise of the Emperor himself. Her plan is thwarted when Aslan sends a party to track another wolf as it flees to the White Witch. Edmund, it seems, is rescued. But in a deeper sense, he is not. Despite his repentance, he is still a sinner under the judgment of the moral law. Aslan has a long talk with Edmund, which we do not witness, as it is no doubt private Confession and Absolution. But a problem remains. In Narnia, God's moral law is represented by the Deep Magic, which states that traitors to Aslan may be slain by the White Witch. We can see the Deep Magic as an expression of God's justice, which cannot be circumvented. For this reason, the Witch is right to demand blood; otherwise, everyone in Narnia would perish.

63. Read Matthew 5:17–18 and Hebrews 9:22. How do these passages show that a holy God will always uphold His Law?

Of course, Aslan must work with the Emperor's Deep Magic. Working against it would be like Jesus rejecting His Father's will in Gethsemane. The Emperor's Law must be upheld, and someone must pay the penalty that Edmund's sin deserves. It may seem odd to readers that only Edmund's sin is mentioned. But Lewis wants us as readers to identify with a believable concrete figure, Edmund, so that we see clearly the wrath we deserve for our sinful natures and actions and so that we more clearly see our desperate need for a savior.

64. Read Psalm 51:1–12. How do these verses reveal the proper understanding of sin that Edmund discovers?

Aslan tells them that he has settled the matter with the Witch, but the children, like Jesus' disciples, do not understand. That night, Susan and Lucy cannot sleep and discover Aslan walking deliberately, sadly, and very tiredly in the woods.

65. Read Matthew 26:36–39. What parallels do you notice?

Aslan stumbles as if carrying a cross, but it is really Edmund's sin that weighs heavily upon him. He is a picture of sadness and loneliness as he feels the alienation, rejection, and wrath that Edmund deserves. Yet he walks willingly into the company of demonic monsters on top of the hill. The Witch calls him a fool, supposing that her triumph is complete. Her wisdom is the wisdom of this world, according to which power always wins.

66. Read 1 Corinthians 1:25–30. What does the Witch fail to understand about divine wisdom?

Aslan is bound, shaved, and mocked, but he offers no resistance and is strangely quiet. At the very point at which he is outwardly most wretched and disfigured, Lucy's eyes of faith see Aslan's bravery. The Witch thinks she can now take Narnia and also go back on her promise by killing Edmund. Aslan is slain on the Stone Table, which suggests both an altar and the cross.

67. Read Isaiah 53:1–7. What parallels do you find?

68. Read Philippians 2:5–8. Why doesn't Aslan use his tremendous power to fight the Witch's monsters? What is the parallel with Christ?

Optional DVD Viewing

You may want to finish viewing *The Lion, the Witch and the Wardrobe* DVD (scenes 18–23). Otherwise, this can be shown at the beginning of the next class.

Words to Remember

But He was wounded for our transgressions; He was crushed for our iniquities; upon Him was the chastisement that brought us peace, and with His stripes we are healed. Isaiah 53:5

For Next Time

To prepare for next week's class, all participants should finish *The Lion, the Witch and the Wardrobe* (chapters 15–17). Some important questions to think about are these:
1. What do we learn about the Deeper Magic?
2. How is Edmund transformed by his justification?
3. What is significant about the way Aslan revives those turned to stone?
4. In what ways would you expect the Pevensie children to be changed on our side of the wardrobe?

A Deeper Magic Still

For a time, it seems that the Witch has triumphed. She rushes off to defeat the remainder of Aslan's army, which symbolizes the Church. Meanwhile, Susan and Lucy grieve over Aslan's lifeless body. They feel cold and empty, believing that they have lost their dearest friend and the one in whom they had come to place all of their hope. There is a vacuum in their soul without Aslan, and they cry until they reach a kind of quietness. Then they feel one of the stages of grief later described by Lewis in *A Grief Observed*: indifference to ordinary life. This is a feeling not that nothing really would happen, but that nothing matters without the one in whom "all things hold together" (Colossians 1:17).

But then there are signs of a change. The mice gnaw through Aslan's cords. The sky gets lighter, yet one star is still visible before dawn. This suggests the morning star, which tells us that the sun is about to rise. The sun that lights our earth is a figure for the Son of God, who shines the light of God's love into a world darkened by sin. Then the Stone Table, on which the Deep Magic is inscribed, audibly cracks. When the children look, Aslan is no longer there. They ask if it is more magic and hear Aslan's voice say "Yes!" When they turn around, they see Aslan alive again, brilliant, larger than life, and physically restored to an even greater glory.

69. Read Mark 15:38; 16:4; Hebrews 10; and Romans 8:1–4. What interpretations do these verses suggest for the cracking of the Stone Table?

Aslan the Glorious

When the children first see Aslan, they naturally cannot believe their eyes. We do not routinely witness dead people rising again. The children even wonder if Aslan had really died. Of course he had, past tense; he was dead but is not now. Susan cannot help thinking that she must be seeing a ghost, but he reassures her of his corporeal solidity. Yet though Aslan has a real living body (his resurrection is not merely spiritual), it is a glorified body, larger and even more full of life.

70. Read 1 Corinthians 15:42–49. What does Paul tell us is different about the resurrection body?

71. Read Luke 24:36–43. How does Jesus reassure His disciples that He is not a ghost?

In the last session, we saw Aslan as the suffering servant, emptying himself of divine power and taking all the wrath and rejection that our sins deserve. Now that he has completed his task, we see Aslan the glorious, the exalted. But how is this possible? Aslan explains that the Witch only knew the Deep Magic, the Law that was built into creation. But there is a Deeper Magic still. Even before creation, our God was a God of love and, knowing that our world would fall into sin, already made provision to save us. Deeper than the Law, which condemns fallen humankind to hell, is the Gospel that God freely chose to send His only Son to die for our sins so that those who believe in Him will not be condemned but have eternal life (John 3:16). God's justice is never compromised, but His love and mercy go deeper.

72. Read Romans 8:1–4. How do the Deep Magic and the Deeper Magic compare with "the law of sin and death" and "the law of the Spirit of life"?

There is a wonderful, joyous frolic with Lucy and Susan trying to catch Aslan that seems like a foretaste of heaven itself. Yet there is work to be done. Having withheld his divine power when slain on the

Stone Table, glorious Aslan now holds nothing back. He roars so powerfully that the trees blow flat, reminding us that Christ is Lord of all creation. When he reaches the Witch's castle, Aslan flies over the wall. Clearly, Aslan's glorified body is no longer subject to the limitations of an ordinary lion.

73. Read John 20:19 and Luke 24:31. How is our risen Lord's body different from an ordinary man's?

Aslan revives the statues on the Witch's castle with his breath. The stone statues had been dead, but now they are alive again. This reminds us that God is the Lord and giver of all life. He first breathed life into earth to make man (Genesis 2:7). But if being turned to stone means being enslaved to sin and spiritually dead, it also means that God renews us through the power of the Holy Spirit, which is likened to a life-giving breath. Before Aslan comes, the statues are "deadly white," reminding us of the oppressive, totalitarian regime of the Witch. When creatures are revived, we see an explosion of color, indicating that our true identity and value as individuals is found in Christ. Like Christ, Aslan does not view his subjects as his captives but as brothers and friends: an ordinary lion is delighted to hear Aslan speak of "Us."

74. Read Romans 8:9–11 and Hebrews 2:14–18. What insights do these passages provide on our new life with Christ and His concern for humanity?

Kings and Queens of Narnia

Without Aslan, Peter's army has not fared well. They are not capable of defeating the White Witch by themselves, just as we lack the power to destroy Satan. As Luther tells us in his hymn "A Mighty Fortress," on earth, Satan has no equal. But there is a champion who can vanquish him, Jesus Christ. Aslan throws himself on the White Witch, and she is slain. Peter and Aslan shake hands, symbolizing the peace between God and humankind won by Christ's victory over sin, death, and the devil.

75. Read 2 Corinthians 5:17–21. What do we learn about the peace that God brings to us and that He calls us to share with our brothers and sisters in Christ?

Although the battle is going badly until Aslan appeared, Edmund shows himself a mighty warrior. He knows that the Witch had special powers, and rather than engaging her in conventional combat, he destroys the wand she used to turn people to stone. He is terribly wounded, like a saint of the Early Church who has taken up his cross and followed a sacrificial life. Fortunately, Lucy's elixir heals Edmund of his wound, but that is not the reason he looks like his old self before things had gone wrong at school. If we assume Edmund was baptized but then started to fall away from faith in school, what we are seeing is Edmund's new life in Christ as his faith is restored. Just as Christ takes sinners and makes them heroes of the faith, Aslan knights Edmund on the battlefield.

76. Read Ephesians 2:1–10. How can this be read as a commentary on Edmund in particular? How does it also apply to all Christians?

All of the children have grown into their assigned vocations. By the end of the book, Peter has led a mighty army into battle and really seems to be a king. The new Edmund is a fierce warrior and a changed boy. Lucy and Susan have also been tested and are ready for their coronation. Yet the children are not exceptional superheroes. They are heroes in the sense that by faith all Christians are heroes. They are kings and queens in the sense that all Christians are incorporated into God's royal family.

77. Read James 1:12. How does this reveal a helpful interpretation of the coronation of the Pevensies?

We should take note of the fact that Aslan himself crowns the Pevensie children. Narnia is nothing like a secular society, in which the state is the final authority and source of legitimacy. In Narnia, we see that even human kings and queens are under God's sovereignty. They have more responsibility than their subjects, but they are still stewards charged with upholding God's Law and serving those in their charge.

78. Read Romans 13:1–7 and Hebrews 13:17. What do these verses say about the connection between divine authority and human authorities? Does this mean that human authorities can do as they please?

Taking a closer look, we see that each of the Pevensies is given a significant title: Peter the Magnificent, Susan the Gentle, Edmund the Just, and Lucy the Valiant. As Aslan's prime representative and leader (the high king), Peter reflects Aslan's magnificence. The titles of Susan, Edmund, and Lucy also have scriptural significance.

79. Read Isaiah 28:29; Galatians 5:22–23; Romans 1:17; and Psalm 108:13. How can these four passages be applied to Peter, Susan, Edmund, and Lucy respectively?

Back on This Side of the Wardrobe

In Narnia, the children grow up to be renowned kings and queens who defend Narnia and have many exciting adventures. One of the later Chronicles, *The Horse and His Boy*, which shows how Aslan works providentially to save Narnia from Calormen (a large empire to the south), takes place during the reign of the Pevensies. With so much work to do in Narnia, we might suppose that Aslan called them there to serve out their entire lives. But there is something deeper going on. Before the Pevensie children enter Narnia, their family structure is beginning to break down. Part of the reason Aslan calls the children into Narnia is so that each of the children learns and grows up into his or her true vocation on this side of the wardrobe.

So it is no doubt Aslan who calls the adult Pevensies back through the wardrobe, where they find themselves to be children again, on the same day and hour that they had entered Narnia. However, outside the wardrobe, the children are dressed as they were before they entered the wardrobe. Although they no longer look like royalty, we recall that kings and queens in Narnia remain king and queens in Narnia. The gains of faith that make the Pevensies part of God's royal family are not lost by their return to England. Nor is their growth in vocation.

80. Read Ephesians 4:14–16. What do these verses say about growth in the faith? Do you think the Pevensie children will be different after their time in Narnia?

In Narnia, Peter is called to be the high king. But even in England, he is called into a high office, to be a surrogate father for the younger children. Likewise, Susan the Gentle, queen of Narnia has the no less challenging role of surrogate mother. Edmund, who had been so resentful of his siblings and had desired to usurp their authority, has learned the error of his ways and has been forgiven in Narnia. He has been set free from his egoism and pride to be whom he is called to be: a contented younger brother united in love with his siblings. Perhaps Edmund is called the Just not only because he has been justified, but also because he has learned what it means for people to mind their own business. Lucy, too, no longer fears the scorn and rejection of her siblings. They now have a common faith and a source of unity that transcends their personal projects.

81. Read Ephesians 4:1–6. What resources do Christians have for harmonious and unified families and communities?

In some ways, Narnia is like a dramatic religious experience involving the mental and spiritual conversion of the children. It seems a bit hard for them to return to their ordinary lives. In the same way, adult converts to Christianity often experience a tremendous spiritual high during their conversion and can be disappointed that God does not call them out of the world into some especially spiritual life of devotion and service. Instead, God wants us right here in our ordinary callings of brother and sister, parent and spouse, worker and citizen. Yet all of these roles are sacred vocations to which God Himself calls us. The children may again find the vivid religious experience of Narnia, but they cannot choose it. It is always God who calls.

82. Read Hebrews 12:1–3. Where should the faithful fix their attention to help them follow their vocation?

Words to Remember

May the God of peace who brought again from the dead our Lord Jesus, the great shepherd of the sheep, by the blood of the eternal covenant, equip you with everything good that you may do His will, working in us that which is pleasing in His sight, through Jesus Christ, to whom be glory forever and ever. Amen. Hebrews 13:20–21

Leader Guide

This guide is provided as a "safety net," a place to turn for help in answering questions and for enriching discussion. It will not answer every question raised in your class. Please read it, along with the questions, before class. Consult it in class only after exploring the Bible references and discussing what they teach. Please note the different abilities of your class members. Some will easily find the Bible passages listed in this study; others will struggle. To make participation easier, team up members of the class. For example, if a question asks you to look up several passages, assign one passage to one group, the second to another, and so on. Divide the work! Let participants present the answers they discover.

Each topic is divided into four sections:

Focus introduces key concepts that will be discovered.

Inform guides the participants into Scripture to uncover biblical images and themes in *The Lion, the Witch and the Wardrobe.*

Law critique considers the images and themes in view of God's commands.

Gospel affirmation helps participants understand how those images and themes can be used to point us to God's Son, Jesus Christ.

The Man behind the Books

Objectives

By the power of the Holy Spirit working through God's Word, participants will

- see how the author of The Chronicles of Narnia, C. S. Lewis, was brought to faith in Christ;
- see what motivated Lewis's fervent desire to reach unbelievers; and
- understand the moral and Christian purpose and methodology behind Lewis's use of storytelling.

Opening Worship

Invocation

In the name of the Father, the Son, and the Holy Spirit. Amen.

Readings from God's Word

All these things Jesus said to the crowds in parables; indeed, he said nothing to them without a parable. Matthew 13:34.

But [Jesus] said to him, "A man once gave a great banquet and invited many. And at the time for the banquet he sent his servant to say to those who had been invited, 'Come, for everything is now ready.' But they all alike began to make excuses. The first said to him, 'I have bought a field, and I must go out and see it. Please have me excused.' And another said, 'I have bought five yoke of oxen, and I go to examine them. Please have me excused.' And another said, 'I have married a wife, and therefore I cannot come.' So the servant came and reported these things to his master. Then the master of the house became angry and said to his servant, 'Go out quickly to the streets and the lanes of the city, and bring in the poor and crippled and blind and lame.' And the servant said, 'Sir, what you commanded has been done, and still there is room.' And the master said to the servant, 'Go out to the highways and hedges and compel people to come in, that my house may be filled. For I tell you, none of those men who were invited shall taste my banquet.'" Luke 14:16–24

Opening Prayer

Lord, heavenly Father, open our minds and hearts to the work of your Son, Jesus Christ, as it is revealed in Your Word, the Bible, and is also reflected in the words of faithful servants such as C. S. Lewis. Bless this Bible class, and help us to get to know You better through our study of the biblical images and themes in *The Lion, the Witch and the Wardrobe*. In Jesus' name. Amen.

(Focus)

1. Answers will vary. Lewis's Chronicles are neither an attempt to impose Christian ideas on anyone, nor presented as an alternative to the Bible. The stories embody biblical themes in concrete forms that open people's minds to the biblical worldview and thereby help prepare them for the Bible or Christian instruction if they ever encounter them. By incarnating Christian truths in concrete forms, Lewis allows readers to see and taste them for themselves. Ultimately, however, the power of the stories comes from the Word of God, which is always just under the surface.

2. Lewis is a tremendous lay spokesperson for the Christian faith and perhaps the most eloquent apologist of the twentieth century. It is hard not to revere him as a champion of the Christian faith. However, like Paul, Lewis did not want people to focus on him as a personality. Neither Paul nor Lewis was crucified for us. A faithful Christian brings nothing of self in his or her hands, but it is empty hands that can point to Jesus. We should value Lewis in a similar way to how we value John the Baptist: as a clear and powerful pointer to Christ.

A Reluctant Convert (Inform)

3. When Lewis became a Christian, he was concerned that many others were still held back by the doubts and problems that he had experienced as an atheist. As a child, he thought a valid prayer required a realization that one had prayed well enough. When he saw that the Holy Spirit intercedes for us and that God does not need our works, he shared his insight in the *Screwtape Letters* (letter IV). He had also been perturbed by the problem of evil, thinking that the world

was at odds with him. When he saw why a God who wants children and not automatons allows His creatures to reject His will and why there is evil and suffering in this world, he wrote *The Problem of Pain*.

4. Lewis thought that too many theologians of his day wrote in a highly technical language that simply did not communicate to most ordinary people. As a master of the English language, Lewis realized that he had the gifts to translate theology into the vernacular—into the language and thought forms that people were actually using. It is very important for the Church to have "high" theologians, such as Martin Chemnitz, who can articulate, develop, and defend Christian doctrines with the utmost rigor, to defend the Church against heresy and false doctrine. But it is equally important to have "low" theologians (not low in intelligence, but close to the ground, where ordinary people walk). These low theologians are often laymen who have a sharp sense of the current fashions of speech and thought and know how to present the Gospel in those terms.

5. Peter tells us that all Christians are called to be prepared to defend their faith. This does not mean everyone has to be an expert "Bible answer man." God provides numerous vocations, and each is an avenue for witness. Wherever God has placed us, we are called to defend the faith against objections and attacks and show its relevance to how we do our work. Paul emphasizes both a negative and a positive role for apologetics. We need to refute arguments and world-views that oppose Christ and show how all correct thought can be obedient to Christ. Answers may vary on whether apologetics is neglected. The author of this Bible study believes it is; it should be restored to its proper place as one of the major branches of theology alongside homiletics and systematic theology. The fact that so many Christians are being taken in by such works as *The Da Vinci Code* indicates that many Christians are *not* ready to defend their faith.

Baptizing the Imagination (Law Critique)

6. The Bible tells us that God inscribed the moral law on the hearts of all people. In that sense it is a natural law, part of general revelation, and not something someone needs the Bible to discern. This is why Paul could call people who knew nothing of Christ to repentance. Nonetheless, the natural person wants to be his or her own god and make his or her own laws. So he or she is always in the business of repressing and burying what he or she knows about the

moral law. God's punishment is to allow those who reject His moral law to suffer the consequences, which may at last bring them to their senses.

7. Jesus told parables because He knew they engaged people at a deeper level than direct instruction. Human beings are very good at interpreting rules in the wrong way or convincing themselves that they have kept them when they really have not (like the Pharisees). We are also good at appreciating an abstraction but not carrying it out. In a story, we see what a doctrine means in concrete terms we can identify with. The story draws us in, convicts us, inspires us, and changes us. If successful, it becomes part of who we are.

8. Answers will vary. The Harry Potter books are very controversial among Christians, but John Granger has argued that there are important Christian themes (see his *Looking for God in Harry Potter*). Tolkien's *The Lord of the Rings* is harder to interpret than Lewis's work, but Gandalf's fall and return are strongly reminiscent of the death and resurrection of Christ. On the other hand, Philip Pullman's works are designed to steer people away from the Savior, to make people happy being part of a material world with no transcendent hope.

Past Watchful Dragons (Gospel Affirmation)

9. Nathan shows us that sinful human beings can see the moral law very clearly when it is someone else who is guilty. David has no difficulty in seeing the sin of the rich man in the story and feels compassion for the poor man. But he had not been able to see that his own sin was just as scarlet or to feel any compassion for Uriah. When Nathan says, "You are the man!" (2 Samuel 12:7), David does see the connection, and because he has condemned the rich man, he sees his own guilt. Very likely, David would have slain Nathan if he had confronted David directly. David needed to see his sin clearly before he would repent with a contrite heart and receive absolution (v. 13).

10. Stories show people's parts and roles. In that way, they help us to see what our vocation is, whom we serve, and how we depend on the vocations of others. Great literature can help to script our lives with a vocabulary of appropriate responses. It can also warn us against missing our cue, saying bad lines, and letting others down.

11. In the prodigal son, we see our sinful desire to walk away from God and to live as we please. Every time we put up a fence

around those things that are "mine," and not God's, we deny the fact that everything we have is a gift of God and that we are called only to be good stewards. As Christians, we can also identify with the elder brother. We are tempted to resent the special treatment given to unbelievers and sinners, forgetting that all of our blessings come from God and that we are called not merely to enjoy them, but also to share them with others, showing our compassion for every lost sheep as Christ did.

12. Everyone can identify with the prodigal son, because all of fallen mankind has walked away from God, taking all the riches of His gifts to squander them on self-centered pursuits. All Christians can identify with the older brother, because we experience complacence, reluctance, and even resentment instead of compassion and zeal when we look out on an unbelieving world. Lewis described himself as a most reluctant convert. Unlike the prodigal son, who at least walked back some way before his father came to meet him, Lewis struggled and looked in every direction for a place to escape. But out of compassion and love, Christ compelled him to come into the kingdom.

Through the Wardrobe

Objectives

By the power of the Holy Spirit working through God's Word, participants will

- understand how God calls Christians into a spiritual battle;
- see how God manifests the infinite and transcendent within the finite and mundane; and
- appreciate how trust and goodness can overcome deception and evil.

Opening Worship

Invocation

In the name of the Father, the Son, and the Holy Spirit. Amen.

Readings from God's Word

Likewise, my brothers, you also have died to the law through the body of Christ, so that you may belong to another, to Him who has been raised from the dead, in order that we may bear fruit for God. For while we were living in the flesh, our sinful passions, aroused by the law, were at work in our members to bear fruit for death. But now we are released from the law, having died to that which held us captive, so that we serve not under the old written code but in the new life of the Spirit. Romans 7:4–6

Finally, all of you, have unity of mind, sympathy, brotherly love, a tender heart, and a humble mind. Do not repay evil for evil or reviling for reviling, but on the contrary, bless, for to this you were called, that you may obtain a blessing. 1 Peter 3:8–9

Opening Prayer

Lord, when You call us, help us to trust like Lucy, and with Your help, to conquer evil with good. Empower us to be Your servants and to confess our faith in truth and in love. In Jesus' name we pray. Amen.

13. The real battle that Christians always face, in peace as well as wartime, is a battle with demonic powers, with the world, the devil, and our sinful flesh. It is a war that cannot be won with human strength or weapons. Rather, we must look to the gifts of the Spirit, which only God can provide. Since Christ has prevailed over Satan, we can be sure that His righteousness, which we receive as a free gift, is sufficient to defend us. Even when we fail, His grace is sufficient, and nothing will separate us from the love of God.

14. The Professor's house, although delightful, is not heaven! However, it has many rooms and opens out into a whole new world, just as the Father's house is heaven itself.

The Meaning of the Wardrobe (Inform)

15. These passages remind the Christian to keep his or her feet on the ground. Even though he was the greatest evangelist of the Early Church, Paul stuck to his tent-making. Likewise, we are called to serve and witness to our neighbor in our ordinary vocations and to bear the crosses that our calling imposes on us. Our refuge is always in Christ, but it is not an escape from the hardships of this world.

16. God calls us to be where we find ourselves. If we have gifts and a station at which we can use those gifts to serve people in God-pleasing ways, this is our calling. Only if we lack the gifts or no one can be served or the work is contrary to God's Law are we called away to new endeavors. It is far truer to say that the office controls and shapes the office holder than the reverse. On account of their offices, doctors, lawyers, politicians, and plumbers are all required to act with fairness and concern for those in their charge, even if it goes against their personal interest, and we hold them accountable if they fail to do so.

17. Christ is He through whom all things were made, the Creator and Sustainer of the entire universe. Yet He also entered our world and became a human being, like the creator of a play writing himself in as a character of that play. When creation fell, the agent of creation stepped in to become the agent of redemption, shedding His blood for all of our sins. We do not have a distant, deistic creator who is unconcerned about his creation, but a loving God who is intimately concerned with the well-being of His creatures.

18. For a sinful human being, the presence of the holy creates fear. We see our own inadequacies more clearly and know that we fall short of God's perfect standard. Yet our God is not only holy, but also compassionate. Though we deserve judgment and death, He tells us not to be afraid, for Christ has been victorious over death and has taken away the condemnation of the Law so that we may enjoy eternal life in heaven.

19. Becoming a Christian is like shutting a door forever on the futile ways of the old Adam. Lewis expresses our human reluctance to let go of our old sinful selves and to be reborn as new people in Christ. He had always looked for an escape route if religious commitment became too much to bear.

Trust, Deception, and Goodness (Law Critique)

20. The natural person does not want to die. The verses from Romans explain that Baptism means death for the old Adam, that becoming a Christian means being joined in death with Christ so that we may be united in His new life. Even those who do hear the Gospel may not understand it or may not have been properly prepared by the Law so that it grows and flourishes. Or a person may fall away through the distractions of worldly concerns. The Law must do its work, breaking our hard hearts and preparing them like soil so that the seed of the Gospel grows and flourishes.

21. Those in league with the devil may disguise themselves as Christ's representatives. Liberal bishops and professors of religious studies often present themselves as Christians while undermining the faith. Wolves in sheep's clothing are dangerous to those weak in their faith. American society so emphasizes getting along and never being dogmatic that pious but doctrinally unsound claims are often embraced uncritically. Whole church bodies can abandon the authority of Scripture in favor of politically correct ideology, and many seem unaware that it has already happened. Good shepherds have the thankless but essential task of exposing the errors of their wayward colleagues.

22. Lucy shows only kindness and compassion to Mr. Tumnus even though he had betrayed her and was planning to kidnap her. While Mr. Tumnus is faithless and deceitful, Lucy is faithful and truthful. When Christ saved us, He did not wait for us to be good. While we were still sinners, He showed His love for us by dying for

us (Romans 5:8). Lucy reflects the same attitude to Mr. Tumnus. She does not wait for him to be good to show him kindness. Lucy's goodness awakens Mr. Tumnus's conscience, and he sees his sin clearly, suffering the "burning coals" of guilt and contrition. As Christ's love calls us to repentance, Lucy's love changes Mr. Tumnus's heart so that he turns away from his sins.

23. Jesus lays the heaviest charge against those, such as the White Witch, who knowingly cause others to sin. All sins are taken very seriously. None of them is acceptable to God. All require repentance. Yet all can be forgiven. As Christ offers forgiveness for the sins of all humankind, we should always be ready to forgive those who sin against us and repent. In calling someone to repentance, it is easy for us to be harsh and self-righteous, which tends to promote defensive and evasive reactions. A gentler approach may be more effective. We easily forget that goodness and kindness can serve as a mirror to awaken someone else to his or her sin.

Edmund and the Wardrobe (Gospel Affirmation)

24. Lucy is like the women who saw the empty tomb and the angels proclaiming the risen Christ in that she has a dramatic, personal religious experience that the other children have not had. The others are like the two men on the road to Emmaus in that, though they have heard the Gospel, they have only half-believed it and now seem inclined to disbelieve it. Just as the men think their hope in a risen Savior has been dashed, the children see only a dead-end, the wooden back of the wardrobe.

25. Lucy, like Paul, must endure the accusation of insanity. Lucy, like Paul, must stick to the truth of revelation no matter how hostile the reaction to it. All Christians are called to proclaim the truth of Christ's death and resurrection no matter how much ridicule is heaped on them by secularists, skeptics, fashionable celebrities, and worldlings.

26. The White Witch is very white and even beautiful, like an angel of light. The devil is not only attractive, but he also makes himself appear good and holy to deceive the unwary. The White Witch's sleigh is pulled by reindeer, just like Father Christmas's, reinforcing the deception. While Father Christmas brings undeserved gifts, reminding us of God's grace, the White Witch takes people away and turns them into stone (a sort of anti-Santa!). So it is important to test

the spirits (1 John 4:1–6) and to judge people by the fruits they produce, a task for which Edmund is ill-equipped.

Faith, Doubt, and Logic

Objectives

By the power of the Holy Spirit working through God's Word, participants will

- understand the allure of temptation and the addictive power of sin;
- see how secularism truncates the proper use of logic and how a Christian can use logic to defend his or her faith; and
- perceive how Lewis evokes the biblical truth that Christians are called into a royal priesthood.

Opening Worship

Invocation

In the name of the Father, the Son, and the Holy Spirit. Amen.

Readings from God's Word

They exchanged the truth about God for a lie and worshiped and served the creature rather than the Creator, who is blessed forever. Romans 1:25

Trust in the LORD with all your heart, and do not lean on your own understanding. In all your ways acknowledge Him, and He will make straight your paths. Proverbs 3:5–6

This is the message we have heard from Him and proclaim to you, that God is light, and in Him is no darkness at all. If we say we have fellowship with Him while we walk in darkness, we lie and do not practice the truth. But if we walk in the light, as He is in the light, we have fellowship with one another, and the blood of Jesus His Son cleanses us from all sin. 1 John 1:5–7

Opening Prayer

Lord, heavenly Father, help us to see that reason is a powerful gift that may be used either to attack or uphold the faith. Inspire us to use reason as a servant of our faith and not a judge, so that we may be led into Your truth. As we see Edmund go wrong, open our eyes to the ways that we are tempted to do likewise, and give us the strength to turn away from darkness and into Your gracious light. In Jesus' name. Amen.

(Focus)

27. Peter tells Christians to wake up! We need to be self-controlled, watching and curbing our sinful tendencies, and we need to be aware of our vulnerabilities and able to identify the many sources of temptation that surround us. The devil seems only to offer pleasure and power, but in reality he wants to enslave and consume us, devouring our souls. We are called to stand firm in the faith, taking comfort from the fact that many Christians around the world and throughout history have endured the same trials. Indeed, the persecuted Church in Africa and Asia is currently suffering hardships we can scarcely imagine yet remains firm in its faith.

Turkish Delight (Inform)

28. As soon as Eve has been tempted by Satan, the forbidden fruit seems more attractive. This is partly its appearance but also its association with wisdom and power. What fuels the desire for the fruit is the thirst to usurp God's authority and to be our own god. Likewise, what lies behind Edmund's craving for Turkish delight is the desire to throw off the legitimate authority of his siblings and everyone else and to assert his independence and ultimate power as king of Narnia, beholden to no-one, not even Aslan.

29. The essence of Edmund's sin is the natural person's craving to possess and control the things of this world, to reject his status as a steward of God's gifts in favor of the fantasy that he is lord and master of reality. These desires come from the world through the prince of this world, Satan. They are deceitful desires because they make us, like Tolkein's Gollum in *The Lord of the Rings*, claim, "Mine! My own . . . My precious!" of things that are God's alone. In its utter rejection of God, the wages of this sin are death. The things of this world are all passing away and cannot save. To put our trust in the treasure of this world is to be eternally bankrupt, destined for destruction. The natural person can never escape the vicious cycle of self-love and rejection of God unless God Himself breaks through and sets the person free.

30. Turkish delight symbolizes the worldly wisdom that the natural person craves. This wisdom focuses on what it takes to get ahead, to assert ones superiority over others. It is motivated by "jealousy and selfish ambition" (James 3:14), and can understand progress only in terms of the vicious struggle for power. It is boastful of accomplishments when credit should be given to God; it suppresses the truth and leads to every kind of conflict and disorder as self-centered wills compete for supremacy. By contrast, heavenly wisdom comes from realizing that God is at peace with us through Christ and that He has already done everything necessary for us to get ahead in eternity. This sets us free from the need to struggle for a vain and fleeting supremacy in this world. Because God has shown these qualities to us, we also can be "peaceable, gentle, open to reason, full of mercy and good fruit, impartial and sincere" (v. 17).

31. The devil makes people liars because he is the ultimate source of all lies (the father of lies). The big lie behind them all is the lie that humans do not need God but can become gods themselves. Every rejection of God's Law, every assertion of independence and ownership, every excuse we make, every sin we commit, every lie we tell to cover up those sins, all of these stem from this one big lie.

Logic! (Law Critique)

32. A secular worldview rejects the Spirit of God. Only this Spirit can break through the natural person's futile attempts to find ultimate meaning in the temporal and mundane and show him or her that the source of meaning, even of mundane objects, is God. We are not a biochemical accident, but creatures of God. Morality is not a human convention, but God's Law. Work is not merely a profession, but a calling from God to serve others. These claims are all foolishness to the natural person but are revealed to the person of faith by the Word and the Holy Spirit.

33. Thomas learns that the risen Christ has a real body that can be detected by our ordinary senses. Of course, it is never evidence alone that makes someone trust in their heart. Recall that the Pharisees witnessed Christ's miracles yet did not believe. It is the Holy Spirit that calls Thomas to say, "My Lord and my God!" But the testimony of his senses shows that the Christian faith is a faith founded on fact, not a subjective private experience.

34. Paul emphasizes that there are many living witnesses of the risen Christ. The force of Paul's assertion is that if someone doubted his testimony they could go and ask someone else. While countless other religions offer experiences, rituals, and rules, only Christianity can make the case that its documents are a historically sound account of God acting in history to save humankind.

A Royal Calling (Gospel Affirmation)

35. The banquet tells us that our heavenly Father calls people into the kingdom who have no natural power to get there. We are all poor—having nothing to offer God, and we are all crippled by sin, spiritually blind and maimed, but through the Gospel He calls us into paradise on account of the work of Christ. Indeed, because we are by nature slaves to sin, He compels us to come in, but His compulsion is liberation from the law of sin and death. Lewis, like all of us, needed to be liberated from himself, from his overwhelming desire to control his own destiny and to live without divine interference.

36. On one level, the coats reflect the way that, by faith, sinful humankind is clothed with Christ's righteousness. But Peter tells us more. When we are clothed with Christ, we become royalty, adopted members of God's royal family. All of this is suggested by the fur coats that protect the children against the Witch's winter (as Christ's righteousness shields us from the devil) and that look like royal robes—because they are.

37. Christians grow up by being called to serve in Christ's body. As the body grows and people serve and are served by others, unity emerges. Those in the body of Christ grow up into Christ the head, the source of life who draws us and nourishes us and builds us up "when each part is working properly" (Ephesians 4:16).

38. Our reason often cannot tell us who or what to trust. We need to see God's will and what is good with the spiritual discernment of the eyes of faith. Leaders who are too cautious and rely only on what they can be sure of by reason will not succeed in their vocation but be paralyzed by indecision and doubt.

Aslan Is on the Move

Objectives

By the power of the Holy Spirit working through God's Word, participants will

- see how faith opens our eyes and hearts and sustains the hope of those who endure trials patiently;
- understand the aptness of Lewis's choice of a lion to represent the king and savior of Narnia; and
- discern the difference between the self-deception of sin, which tries to go it alone without God, and the wonderful gifts God provides His faithful servants so they may carry out their assigned work.

Opening Worship

Invocation

In the name of the Father, the Son, and the Holy Spirit. Amen.

Readings from God's Word

Those who live according to the flesh set their minds on the things of the flesh, but those who live according to the Spirit set their minds on the things of the Spirit. To set the mind on the flesh is death, but to set the mind on the Spirit is life and peace. For the mind that is set on the flesh is hostile to God, for it does not submit to God's law; indeed it cannot. Romans 8:5–7

Behold, I am doing a new thing: now it springs forth, do you not perceive it? I will make a way in the wilderness and rivers in the desert. Isaiah 43:19

Opening Prayer

Lord, heavenly Father, help us to discern our natural and spiritual gifts, to accept them with gratitude and to use them wisely in our various callings. We thank You and praise You for the most precious gift of all, Your Son, Jesus Christ, through whom we pray. Amen.

(Focus)

39. If Aslan is interpreted as the name of God and reports of Aslan's works are the Word of God, we can expect Mr. Beaver's words to have power. The Word of God is alive; it changes people's hearts; it judges our inmost thoughts and convicts us of sin; it tells us the good news of a Savior. Although the children are afraid of Aslan on account of their sin, the report of his coming evokes joy like the coming springtime, which is greeted as good news.

40. The key to the reaction to Aslan, as well as to Christ, is faith. Those children who believe that Aslan is their savior see him in his true light as a refuge from sin and condemnation. But those who prefer to stay in their sins cannot bear the light of his judgment, which exposes, judges, and condemns them because they refuse to accept their need for a savior. Edmund is still in bondage to sin and so is dispossessed from the Emperor's family. Only Aslan can set him free, but Edmund resents and rejects any authority or power beyond his own. The cost of the freedom to do as he pleases is Edmund's slavery to sin and the Witch.

The Last Prophets and the Lion of Judah (Inform)

41. Edmund's mind is consumed by what his sinful nature desires: power, wealth, and revenge, but his siblings have been drawn to Aslan and surrender their wills to his. While Edmund can think only of imposing his will on others, his siblings are set free to do Aslan's will. Likewise, we are drawn by the Holy Spirit to Christ.

42. Zechariah and Simeon are filled with joy to see with their own eyes how God fulfills the promises they and the prophets before them had so long believed and hoped for. Likewise, the Beavers rejoice to see the prophecies of Narnia unfold before their eyes.

43. Unbelievers have hearts of stone: cold, hard, spiritually dead, and unable to trust. Believers have hearts of flesh: warm, soft, spiritually alive, and trusting in God. Satan wants spiritually dead slaves and prisoners; God wants sons and daughters to rejoice in the heavenly banquet.

44. The title *Lion of Judah* expresses the wild, irresistible power of God's holiness that no man can tame and all fear. Our God is a God whose will is done with or without our cooperation! His Law opens wounds, showing our sin and calling us to repentance. But the same lion heals those wounds and restores us. Our God is a God of

grace and forgiveness as well as a God of justice and judgment. The *Lion of Judah* is also the *Paschal Lamb*, slain for our sins, who heals us by His wounds.

45. Isaiah shows us that God is completely outside of our control. We cannot tell Him anything He does not know. The most powerful nations all pass away, but the Lord remains. God cannot rightly be compared to anything we fashion, as if He were our creature. He is the sovereign Creator and Sustainer of all things, beholden to no one. He does not grow tired but stands as the eternal source of all human strength. Whatever our achievements, they always trace to God and always fall short of God Himself, who alone remains the same yesterday, today, and forever.

Self-Deception and Betrayal (Law Critique)

46. When Edmund rejects all authority save his own, he rejects God and his brother at the same time. Edmund thinks he is enlightened, but his rejection of the siblings God gave him, people made in the image of God and his own flesh and blood, shows that he is really living in the darkness of self-deception and sin. He is living a lie, claiming to be without sin, and must first be called to recognize, confess, and repent of his sin.

47. God cannot be mocked. Those who ridicule and reject God face only His judgment.

48. Edmund's heart is calloused, he is deaf to Aslan's word, and his eyes are blinded by sin so that he cannot see the truth about Aslan. His siblings have started to understand with their hearts, to hear Aslan's call, and to see their salvation.

49. Sin is based not merely on selfishness, but on deceitful desires. When we sin, we lie to ourselves about our true good, which God provides us, and we put our trust in the empty idols of wealth, power, fame, and pleasures that pass away, none of which have any power to save us. When Christ declares us holy, we start to see the truth. We see that only Christ can save us and that our natural ways of thinking are futile and corrupt. The more Edmund deceives himself into thinking the Witch cares about him and will really give him the world, the further he is willing to go to betray his brother and sisters.

Equipped to Serve (Gospel Affirmation)

50. Scripture values wisdom. Ultimately, the most important wisdom is the wisdom of the Gospel, which is foolishness by human standards. But ordinary prudence, enhanced by spiritual discernment, is an important gift for a Christian's daily life. We Christians need to be shrewd to discern our spiritual enemies—the wolves who would wrest us away from Christ. We should be transformed by the renewing of our mind so that we can see God's will in the confusion of a fallen world. The fact that we should trust Christ with a childlike heart does not exempt us from developing an adult mind capable of repelling challenges to our faith at the highest level.

51. Paul tells us of the belt of God's truth and the breastplate of Christ's righteousness. Peter's gifts may be interpreted as the shield of faith and "the sword of the Spirit, which is the word of God" (Ephesians 6:17). For the other gifts, answers will vary. Susan's horn that can be used to summon help suggests the gift of prayer mentioned in verse 18. Her accurate arrows suggest the Christian's acute awareness of evil. Lucy's healing elixir reminds us that all Christians are called to forgive others and that whoever we forgive God Himself forgives.

52. Paul tells us that we should judge ourselves with humility and accuracy in terms of the gifts God has actually given us, not in terms of gifts that we like to imagine we have or ones that we long for. From a sober perspective, we can see how our gifts play an important role in the body of Christ and also appreciate how we benefit from the gifts of others. We do not have the same gifts, but we all are important for the overall functioning of the body of Christ.

Promise Breakers and Promise Keepers

Objectives

By the power of the Holy Spirit working through God's Word, participants will

- understand the dynamic of repentance;
- see the various ways in which God brings new life to a fallen world; and
- understand how God upheld His Law yet saved us from the condemnation we deserved by sending His Son to fulfill the Law and take our punishment on Himself.

Opening Worship

Invocation

In the name of the Father, the Son, and the Holy Spirit. Amen.

Readings from God's Word

A voice cries: "In the wilderness prepare the way of the LORD; make straight in the desert a highway for our God." Isaiah 40:3

Just as it is appointed for man to die once, and after that comes judgment, so Christ, having been offered once to bear the sins of many, will appear a second time, not to deal with sin but to save those who are eagerly waiting for Him. Hebrews 9:27–28

Opening Prayer

Lord, heavenly Father, help us to see that You alone are the great promise keeper, who looks after us, preserves us, provides for our needs of body and soul, and even provided Your only Son, Jesus Christ, as the complete payment for all of our sins. Thank You for keeping all Your promises that You make to us in Your Word. In Jesus' name. Amen.

(Focus)

53. Heaven and earth will pass away. If our faith is founded on the things of this world, it is a house built on sand. Even if we were to receive the whole world, as Edmund vainly hopes, it would profit us nothing, because our soul would be lost to Satan. But if we build our faith on the rock that is Christ, no calamity, not even the destruction of the whole world, can separate us from the love of God.

Repentance (Inform)

54. Like Judas, Edmund had somehow deceived himself into thinking his betrayal would not lead to disastrous consequences. Edmund had tried to tell himself that the Witch would not do anything too bad to his siblings and is horrified when he learns that she plans to kill them. Now that he realizes she has no intention of granting him power over Narnia, he is no longer blind to the truth about his betrayal of his siblings and Aslan. Likewise, Judas is filled with remorse when he sees that Jesus is condemned, and he confesses his sin of betrayal. Judas throws his payment back in the temple, and Edmund is no longer seized by a craving for more than God has provided. Happily, Edmund, unlike Judas, does not hang himself, for Aslan draws Edmund into faith.

55. In the narrow sense, repentance involves acknowledging our sin and having sorrow over our sin (contrition). But all of this is the work of the Law, which does not make anyone trust in a savior. Repentant people see their need for a savior, but that savior must be proclaimed (the Gospel) to them, and through the power of the Holy Spirit, they may then trust in Christ. John prepared the way by preaching repentance and pointing to Christ.

56. We are all sinful by nature, and human righteousness can never make us acceptable to a holy God. The filthy rags of our righ teousness must be covered by the perfect white robe of Christ's righ teousness.

57. Aslan forgives Peter by his grace, which Peter accepts by faith. When God looks at us, He does not look at our old Adam but sees Christ, our mediator. By faith we cling to God's grace in Christ; Christ alone is our righteousness.

Signs of Change (Law Critique)

58. All of creation is cursed by the fall and waits for the renewal of all things in the new heaven and earth. The transition from winter to spring reminds us that God can bring new life out of a dead world.

59. Joel speaks of the way God restores a land ravaged by locusts, but we may think of the way God brings life to a world ravaged by sin. The autumn and spring rains are a picture of salvation since newness of life comes from above through the waters of Baptism and the transcendent Word of God.

60. Christ is the Bridegroom of the Church, and while He is here, we should celebrate the wedding, the reconciliation of God with humankind. Yet we cannot forget that this peace came at the price of the Bridegroom's precious blood, that our joy was purchased by Christ on the cross.

61. God declares us righteous on account of Christ's righteousness and perfect obedience unto death. Yet, so long as Christians are in their fallen flesh, they will struggle with sin and must lead a life of daily repentance, dying and rising in the renewal of their Baptism.

62. Humans look at the outward appearance: strength, intelligence, popularity, skills, and résumé. But God looks at our heart. Through faith, God provides all manner of gifts that empower us to do His work but are invisible to the world's eyes. From the Early Church until the present, faith has enabled ordinary people to do extraordinary things, proclaiming the truth with the eloquence of the Holy Spirit, standing firm amidst adversity and persecution. The Pevensie children do not look like kings and queens, but Aslan will make them so.

The Deep Magic (Gospel Affirmation)

63. The Gospel does not mean that the Law does not matter. Christ came to fulfill the Law, and it remains in effect. The Law requires that no sin may be forgiven except by the shedding of blood. Our sinful Law-breaking must be paid for. It should be us who pay, but God sent His Son to pay for us.

64. Sin is first an inherited sickness and then a choice. It is, since the fall, our natural state. We are not basically good people who could flourish if only other people would get out of our way. We are lost, sinful enemies of God with no power to turn to Him. We need

God to have mercy on us and create a new heart of flesh in us to replace our natural heart of stone. Edmund realizes for the first time his true need for a savior.

65. Jesus was "very sorrowful, even to death" (Matthew 26:38), bearing the sins of the world and facing the wrath and rejection we deserve. It is a task no one, not even the Son of God, can enjoy, yet He humbly submitted His will to the will of His Father. Likewise, Aslan feels alone and sad, resigned to his appointed suffering and death on behalf of Edmund and all of Narnia.

66. God's wisdom is from above. It is the opposite of worldly wisdom, the wisdom of the Witch. The wisdom of this world comes from below and tries in vain to reach up to heaven and seize the things of God. The wisdom from above reaches down to us to save us. It does not work by human power but through what the world considers weakness. Christ emptied Himself of the use of His divine power and suffered a humiliating death so that the Law no longer condemns those who believe in Him.

67. Christ, like Aslan, does not look beautiful to the world's eyes. Both are "despised and rejected," full of sorrows, and "acquainted with grief" (Isaiah 53:3). Both took upon themselves the sickness and sorrows of others. Both are pierced for the sins of others. Both bring healing through their wounds and peace through their punishment. Like a sheep to the slaughter, Christ, like Aslan, offered no resistance and "opened not His mouth" (v. 7).

68. Aslan can atone for Edmund's sin only if he is slain on the Stone Table. His work requires him to withhold his power. Likewise, Christ was called by God the Father to lay down the use of His divine power and to act as a humble, human servant, suffering and dying for all humankind.

A Deeper Magic Still

Objectives

By the power of the Holy Spirit working through God's Word, participants will

- see the glorious bodily resurrection on the other side of the cross;
- better understand the sense in which all Christians are kings and queens; and
- see how ordinary life is charged with spiritual meaning and purpose.

Opening Worship

Invocation

In the name of the Father, the Son, and the Holy Spirit. Amen.

Readings from God's Word

He is the radiance of the glory of God and the exact imprint of His nature, and He upholds the universe by the word of His power. After making purification for sins, He sat down at the right hand of the Majesty on high, having become as much superior to angels as the name He has inherited is more excellent than theirs. Hebrews 1:3–4

Aspire to live quietly, and to mind your own affairs, and to work with your hands, as we instructed you, so that you may live properly before outsiders and be dependent on no one. 1 Thessalonians 4:11–12

Opening Prayer

Lord, when we think of Your holy Law and of our sin we sometimes despair. Keep our eyes fixed on Jesus, the author and perfecter of our faith, so that we can live in hope, trusting in His righteousness for our salvation. For His name's sake. Amen.

(Focus)

69. The cracking of the Stone Table suggests the rending of the temple curtain on Good Friday. This signifies that, through Christ, Christians can approach God's throne of grace with confidence, without the need for a veil and special sacrifices as in the Old Testament. Again, it suggests the rolling away of the stone and the empty tomb of Easter. Since the table is an altar, it suggests the end of the Old Testament sacrificial system because Christ on the cross made a once-and-for-all sacrifice for the sins of all humankind. Also, since the Deep Magic (the Law of God) is inscribed on the Stone Table, its cracking also signifies the end of the Law's power to condemn those who trust in Christ.

Aslan the Glorious (Inform)

70. The resurrection body is imperishable, glorious, powerful, and sinless. It will be like Christ's resurrection body: physical, but spiritual in the sense that it is fully under the governance of the spirit.

71. Jesus shows His disciples His physical body and allows them to touch Him. He further demonstrates that the resurrection body is physical by eating fish. Likewise, Aslan shows Lucy and Susan that he is a real beast.

72. The Deep Magic by itself is like God's Law by itself: it has power only to condemn us for our sin. But the Deeper Magic is like the Gospel, which forgives us and saves us on account of the righteousness of Christ and His sufferings and death and calls us to faith and new life in Him.

73. Jesus can appear and disappear at any time and place. His glorified body is not limited by the normal laws applying to objects in space and time. Likewise, the risen Aslan can do things no ordinary lion could do.

74. A Christian has a new life, because now Christ Himself is living within him or her. Christ showed His solidarity with human beings by becoming one of us, being made like us in every way, although without sin, so that He could represent all of humanity, take on the sins of the whole world, and offer His mercy to all humankind.

Kings and Queens of Narnia (Law Critique)

75. God made us a new creation by reconciling us to Himself through Christ. Having declared peace on humankind and having forgiven all our sins through Jesus, He calls each of us to live in peace and forgiveness with his or her neighbors.

76. Edmund had been dead in "trespasses and sins" (Ephesians 2:1), disobedient, "carrying out the desires" (v. 3) of his sinful nature, and an object of wrath. But now he has been made alive by grace, and the new Edmund is God's "workmanship, created in Christ Jesus for good works" (v. 10). In just the same way, all Christians are called through Baptism and the Word to die to the old Adam and live a new life obedient to the vocations in the body of Christ that God provides.

77. The Pevensies have persevered under trial, growing up into their vocations through a faith that gives access to a crown of eternal life.

78. All human authority is instituted by God. But leadership is an office of stewardship: leaders are responsible for the welfare of those in their charge. All offices are under God's Law, and all human leaders remain accountable to God.

79. Peter's magnificence reflects the magnificence of God's wisdom. This is fitting, because Peter is the high king and his counsel should reflect the wisdom of the one who called him to the highest office. Susan's gentleness reminds us of the gifts of the Spirit that reflect Christ's loving attitude to us. Edmund is the Just because he has been brought out of death into life by faith: "the just shall live by faith" (Romans 1:17 KJV). Lucy's ability to "do valiantly" (Psalm 108:13) is the courage and heroism born of faith.

Back on This Side of the Wardrobe (Gospel Affirmation)

80. Faith involves growing away from deception to truth, growing up into Christ as we mature in our vocations and build up the body of Christ. Although Lewis does not say so in this book, later we see that the Pevensie children have grown and matured in our world and that they do not leave behind the gains they have made in Narnia.

81. God provides us with humility, gentleness, patience, endurance, and peace. The one body of Christ and the "one God and Father of all" (Ephesians 4:6) provide strength for the unity of families and communities.

82. Christians are not called to figure out every detail of their vocation for themselves, but to keep their eyes fixed on Jesus, the "founder and perfecter of our faith" (Hebrews 12:2). As a sailor who wants to avoid shipwreck should keep his or her eyes fixed on the lighthouse rather than worrying about everything going on aboard ship, we follow our vocations most faithfully when we forget ourselves and see Christ in the neighbor we are called to serve.

Further Up and Further In

On completion of this Bible class, it is hoped that many participants will go on to read or reread the other Chronicles of Narnia and other works by C. S. Lewis. For those who want to do further reading *about* C. S. Lewis's life and works, here is a select bibliography.

Baehr, Ted and James, eds. *Narnia Beckons: The Lion, the Witch and the Wardrobe and Beyond.* Broadman & Holman, 2005.

Bassham, Gregory, and Walls, Jerry, eds. *The Chronicles of Narnia and Philosophy.* Open Court, 2005.

Downing, David C. *Into the Wardrobe.* Jossey Bass, 2005.

Gresham, David. *Jack's Life: A Memory of C. S. Lewis.* Broadman and Holman, 2005.

Jacobs, Alan. *The Narnian: The Life and Imagination of C. S. Lewis.* HarperSanFrancisco, 2005.

Menuge, Angus, ed. *C. S. Lewis: Lightbearer in the Shadowlands.* Crossway Books, 1997.

Mueller, Steven P. *Not a Tame God: Christ in the Writings of C. S. Lewis.* Concordia Publishing House, 2002.

Schakel, Peter. *The Way into Narnia: A Reader's Guide.* Eerdmans, 2005.

Veith, Gene Edward. *The Soul of the Lion, the Witch and the Wardrobe.* Victor, Cook Communications, 2005.

Notes

Notes